WISDO

MIEKE MOSMULLER

WISDOM IS A WOMAN

Novel

OCCIDENT PUBLISHERS

Original title: De wijsheid is een vrouw
Translated by Ruth Franssen
Proofreading by Terry Boardman

ISBN 978-90-75240-00-09
NUR 300
Copyright © Occident Publishers, Baarle Nassau 2015
Internet: www.occident-publishers.com
E-mail: info@occident-publishers.com
Coverdesign: Occident/Mieke Mosmuller
Cover: Ghent Altarpiece, The Lamb of God Ghent, Belgium

A woman was sitting on a bench in the spring sun. The apple tree cast a shade, because of which she constantly moved over a little. It was too chilly to think of the cool of the shade as pleasant. She looked over to the hills. In the distance was a farm; people would be living there – otherwise there was nobody to see. On Sundays it was always busy here; people often went for a walk. South Limburg on a Thursday afternoon... seemed deserted.

She shivered. Deserted. One could feel so intensely lonely. What is a human life? You have a body, and from the moment – sooner or later – that you become aware of the temporary nature of it, there is the prevailing question: what is a human life? Is it only the body that is born and is determined by ambient conditions? What does dying mean then? If you observe what is inside you, very honestly and fearlessly, shouldn't you admit that there is nothing else inside you than what you have ever taken in with your senses? Is it not consistent to think... that with the dying of the body also the ability to observe and experience dies? If only there would be something to find, somewhere in our experience, that does *not* come from the senses...

7

Here she sat, and felt the desertion. She felt it so strongly because of the deserted spring landscape. If she had stayed at home, in her busy daily life, there would have been no opportunity to feel this loneliness. But then the landscape would have been here without being experienced. She sighed deeply. What is a human being...?

The wind's warm breath blew gently. It gave her a feeling of comfort. A fresh spring, but a warm wind. Above her in the blossoming branches... a light blue sky. Light pink, light blue. The white light caressed the leaves that appeared pink in its touch. Where you are born, you are at home. They were born here, she and her twin sister, in the farthest south of the country, on a farm with apple trees in bloom.

Each Monday the white laundry waved on long clothes lines. Apples and cherries - her parents sold the apples and the cherries in large buckets and cases for two guilders a bucket. You are a happy person if your senses have enjoyed such impressions as a child. You can always come back to them in your memory. No paving-stones, cars, flats and trams, but cherry trees and waving white laundry, stiff from the starch, later freshly ironed on the beds. The scent of the henhouse, the eggs picked up every morning. The dunghill at the back.... Here, in the far distance, was a farm like that, where everything would be different now. You could not live from apples and cherries, or prunes anymore. The farm was sold for almost a million when her parents died. Who would be able to sell prunes then...? What is a human life...? It consists of sadness. Everything that lives in the senses is there to die – at last. At the peak of beauty dying begins.

She looked up to the apple blossom. In its full bloom she saw the beginnings of withering, here and there. Like one sees in a human life, more and more. Valuable in the beauty of youth – but already then on its way to loss. Time only brings loss, no victory. Loss of youth, loss of bloom. This is how one sees the human being.

She shivered and jumped to her feet but nevertheless got cold. She took a deep breath. She resolutely shook her head, as if to deny her thought. No, a human being is not like that. A human being wins with time, by waking up. In the heart of withering, the fruit grows, also in nature.... True beauty is wisdom – and that can not yet be present in youth.

*

On a bench in the spring sun a woman was looking at the waves on the beach. A heavy wind was blowing that made the waves roll over high. She got up and walked down the stairs, to the beach. She looked for a chair behind glass, away from the wind. She felt her ripe body with pleasure, which always drew the attention of men. She liked these looks of pleasure and she always looked right back. Insecurity? She was not familiar with that weakness. She hated weakness and laughed at all men and women for it. Everyone – accept her twin sister, who was the most insecure human being she knew. No, she might be the most secure...

9

you just did not know with her. She was reserved, that she was....

The spring sun was pleasantly warm, away from the wind. She ordered a cappuccino, which had by then become commonplace. She felt pleasantly warm and untied the buttons of her jacket. She pushed her black hair out of her face and looked around. She loved the sea and the beach, even in Scheveningen, where the wind blows too hard most of the time. She loved the airs, the waves, the sand... power without life. Pure power, ebb and flow, wind, storm. Here the mysterious plant life was not to be found. You could see people with dogs and people behind a cup of cappuccino or a glass of beer. That is why she had become a surgeon and not an internist. You work in internal processes, with the knife... and not in those incomprehensible functions of the body, where you can only take a spot sample. She did not care for music; it could not keep her attention at all. Architecture and sculpture could set her on fire, while a symphony bored her...

Life is beautiful when you are *strong* – and you happen to be strong at the expense of the weaker ones. Opposite her was a woman of her age, an ugly woman. She hated ugly women, they were weak too, they did not know how to present themselves. Contempt was still a minor indication; she *hated* ugliness. Her sister said to her:

'Why do you take credit for your beauty and intelligence? They are not *your* merits, are they? You just *have* them, they're your good fortune, that's all.'

'I don't only *have* them, I also use them, I cultivate them, I enjoy them. It's not only about the shapes that are perfect, it's also pleasure and nerve, they make me beautiful and intelligent. I do that myself, little sister!'

They were binovular twins, they were alike in nothing. But they had parents, a pregnancy, a youth, a life in common – that was *a lot*. Actually, there was only *one* person in the world to whose opinion she attached value: the opinion of her sister. Because of that opinion she now and then got round to think, philosophize a little, like now behind a window-glass in the spring sun on the beach at Scheveningen. People are essentially evil, depraved. A bestial urge to survival of the fittest prevails. Well, fit she certainly was!

She called for the waiter and paid. They were always at her feet because she was intentionally unfriendly. While he took the cup away nervously, she got up, irritated, and buttoned up her coat. She walked straight out in the direction of the waves. The sand got in her shoes, but she did not care. The wind embraced her powerfully and messed up her hair. She braced her power firmly against the wind.

Those who walk towards the truth
Walk alone
No one can be
another's travelling companion.

Christian Morgenstern (1871-1914)

They were born on a farm with an orchard of great fruit trees, around the middle of the last century. Their mother had a couple of miscarriages before she could hold a pregnancy. She became very heavy and the doctor thought to feel two little heads.... Thus two girls were born within the hour. They screamed as loudly as each other, but the resemblance stopped there...

Their father was standing there quietly, he still had his hat on his head. In the tension he forgot to take it off – until the second baby was born. Then he took it off to thank God.

Her father was a quiet, considerate man. From early morning until late in the evening he worked in the garden, but he loved the girls above all. If he stood on top of a ladder to pluck apples and he heard a child's voice, he came down off his ladder cautiously and lifted the girl high up in the air. He was a devout man, steeped with a deep, old fashioned faith. To be absent on Sunday from Holy Mass was a cardinal sin, and so one he did not commit. Like a good Catholic, he did not read the holy scripture, but let himself be taught from the gospel that was read aloud on Sundays. In everything he endeavoured to be moderate, except in his

13

love for his wife and daughters. When his father became a widower, he took him into his house....

He was a quiet man, but he saw and heard everything. To him life was a great prayer, filled with concern. With softness he plucked his apples and cherries, with softness he put them in buckets and chests. With softness he judged his fellow man.

A bit further off was another farm, also with fruit trees, and with a family with six children. The girls went playing there often and were astonished how *different* everything was there. The farmer never plucked his own fruit, but had seasonal fruitpickers to do it. He walked around in his overalls and wooden shoes like their father, a hat on his head. And just like their father, he was in church every Sunday in a decent suit and prayed the Lord's Prayer. But for lunch on that same Sunday he had personally wrung a chicken's or a rabbit's neck the day before. And if the guard-dog got ill he killed it with his old military gun. When the children had been naughty, they got a beating with the carpet-beater, which hung threateningly on a hook in the scullery. She, the youngest of the twins, always became a little nauseous if she looked at it, and also when she ran into the farmer, although he was always very friendly to her. Often she could not eat in the evening and her father looked at her, concerned. One night, when she was going to bed, he asked her:

'What's wrong, my child, what's the matter with you?'

It was never hard to explain to him what you were feeling.

'I get sick when I'm at the neighbours. I am afraid of that father, he's so harsh and rough. You would never kill our chickens or rabbits to eat them... I find it so scary!'

He sat on the rim of her bed; her sister was still washing herself. She did not want *her* to hear it! She would laugh at her! But father caressed her hair softly and said:

'It is nature, sweet child. It is very normal that a farmer butchers his animals, it is his profession.'

'He's a fruit farmer, just like you are. You would never do that!'

'Perhaps that's weakness... I simply can't do it. I attach myself too much to the animals – let them just live and die. I can't do it. But you can't judge him for that. He has a lot of mouths to feed; he has many worries.'

'But... I also find it scary that the children are beaten. That isn't allowed, is it?!

You aren't allowed to kick and hit, even if you are a father?'

'He must keep six of those rascals quiet; that's something different from two good girls. Come, say a prayer and go to sleep.'

She got out of her bed to say her evening prayer on her knees.

With the same patience he waited until her sister said her prayer and was lying under the sheets. Then he kissed them and left the room. She did not understand it very well. How could something be good and bad at the same time? She still felt not right.

'I've heard you talking to dad!' whispered her sister mocking. 'You're a scaredy-cat! Tomorrow I'm going to tell eve-

15

rybody! That you're scared of farmer Erens. We'll all laugh at you!'

She turned over to her side. Her nausea was gone. She said out loud:

'Go ahead! Farmer Erens likes me far more than he likes you. Watch out that he doesn't catch you!'

She might be good and shy – she was not afraid of her sister, never. She always tried to domineer because she was not even an hour older than her. She liked to do all kinds of things that were not allowed – and *she* had to play along with that. 'Do as I tell you to, I'm the oldest.' But she was never intimidated by her. She only played along when she wanted to, and otherwise simply did not.

'Goodnight' sounded the little voice of the oldest to make it up to her.

'Till tomorrow.' She said.

After school she looked for her father, who was working in the garden.

'Dad, how can something be good *and* bad at the same time?'

He put his shovel down and sat with her on a tree stump.

'What do you mean, child?'

His blue eyes looked at her gently. She had never seen him angry, or irritated.

'I compare farmer Erens to you. A man should be like you. You're the best fruit farmer in the whole world and you're good to everything that lives. But you don't object to farmer Erens killing animals and hurting children.'

'Should I really object to that? Do you think that?'

16

She thought about it for a little while and shook her head.

'You never object to anything.'

He chuckled.

'Rotten apples and cherries!'

'Is farmer Erens not a 'rotten' man?'

'I understand that he is the way he is, child. If you understand, it isn't necessary to approve or object to something.'

'Aren't you scared of him?'

'I get on well with him. Very well. It's nature, child. He's closer to nature than I am.'

'Is there no good and bad in nature, then?'

'Well...' said father, uncertain. 'You're asking me something there. I don't believe there is, no. You can't blame a lion for devouring his prey. Farmer Erens is a farmer, he's grown up like that, he acts the way he is. Sometimes he's friendly, sometimes he's angry. And butchering animals is part of his being farmer. You must look at that in a different way.'

'But he hurts his children!'

'For some children there's no harm in that.'

'We're bad sometimes too!' She thought about her sister, who liked to do everything that God has forbidden.

Father smiled at her, shaking his head.

'Dear child, I cannot do it! I can't raise my hand against a living being. But neither can I judge a fellow man.' He got up and kissed her on her head.' So, and now I'm going to start working again!'

She walked inside, to her mother. She was a large, red cheeked, pleasant lady, who wore an apron. She was always

17

busy washing, ironing, cooking, baking, making jam, bottling fruit and more. She was a happy woman, because she was surrounded with love.

She sat at the kitchen table to watch her mother peeling potatoes.

'Mother? Is father an ordinary man?'

She burst into a cordial laugh.

'Ordinary? No, definitely not.'

'Why not?'

Mother became serious. She put her peeler down and wiped her hands on her apron.

'Your father... is a distinguished man, who happens to be born as a farmer. Perhaps it should be like this. Simple, good and gentle, that's your father. There is no other like him, child, remember that well. No other. And your mother knows that, I've been living with him for a long time already.'

'But... if there's no other like him – isn't he very lonely then?'

'Saintly people are always lonely... they are misunderstood by everyone, but they understand everyone else.'

'Is father saintly?'

'*I* think he is, child. But I'm not the pope, am I? It's just a feeling....'

Satisfied, she got up and walked outside, looking for her sister to play with.

*

She, the eldest of the twins, had the same memories of

her youth, and still they were also very different.

Her father was a strong man, you could never make him out very well. It seemed like he allowed everything, and yet you were on your guard for him. She liked to test the limits, in order to be on the border of the tolerable and cross that border a little bit. Her friend on the Erens farm was her companion in this, and both of them loved to try out just what was forbidden. If they were found out, Jet just got an honest whipping on her backside, but she... *she* had to face her parents. There was no hitting, no punishment, you were not even rejected. You just had to face your father and then you rejected yourself, you could not do otherwise. Jet could gossip about her father and say that he had hit her and that he was a miserable father. She could not do that, because she loved her father, like she also loved her good, fussy sister. They always understood everything and before such understanding, you are helpless.... Nevertheless, it did not restrain her from climbing high trees – and falling out and breaking her arm; from not looking before she leapt, and almost drowned. And when she got bigger and her body became more and more beautiful, she kissed the under-gardener and the baker's son, while her sister always knew that she did that but never considered doing it herself.

She was lazy in every respect. She was given a clear notion by God, but she did not use it; she *enjoyed* it. With her mocking cleverness she put everyone's backs up, and in her healthy body she experienced a blissful pleasure. That pleasure asked to be touched and she soon found the way to get boys to do that. Together with Jet she arranged for dates at the crucifix along the field-track and giggling, they hid in the wheat field, a little apart from each other, to appear again together and go home innocently. Farmer Erens suspected nothing of it, but her father *knew* and she felt it.

He told her how boys and girls kiss each other in the spring time and how girls are always the suckers at last when they go too far.... He told her just like that, without a reason. She knew that he was warning her, and she warned Jet. She never went too far again from that moment on, but Jet believed that it would not be so bad. Until she got pregnant and her father beat her, which caused her to have a miscarriage. And so, just like that, everything was solved after all....

The village doctor was the most interesting man in her life. She was a healthy child and seldom had to visit him, but one day she got a swollen red toe that became more and more painful. At first she tried to hide the pain, but walking became harder and harder and inevitably the moment came when her father saw it and drove her to the clinic. On the farmstead there was a shiny polished Opel Rekord, its seats furnished with red imitation leather. It slightly smelled of petrol, and she enjoyed that smell. The car was not often used, only for a trip on a Sunday afternoon or a trip to the big city. Now father sat behind the wheel, and she was allowed to sit next to him on the front seat – for she could not walk because of the pain!

She felt a not-inconvenient tension while she was waiting for her turn. In the consulting-room the chest with instruments stood out the most.... Syringes, needles, shiny boxes, bottles with iodine and so on. The doctor applied a bandage and instructed her to keep it wet. She had to lift her leg high and come back the next day.

Somewhat disappointed she went back home. She had expected more action from a doctor!

The infection got worse, and the next day she even felt a little ill. The doctor took her pulse, looked at her, concerned, and then he cast a quick look at her toe.

'The nail has to come off!' he said apologetically. 'It's grown into your toe and the flesh is inflamed. Come and sit here.'

The assistant joined them and she looked with her heart in her mouth at all the preparations. A table with a white cloth on it, shiny instruments, an injection needle.... A strong girl of fourteen years old was not scared by that – and *she* even thought it was exciting. An orange rubber tape was pulled around her toe; the doctor gave her an anaesthetic and got to work. She was not able to see what he was doing and her father was next to her with her hand in his. She actually had only *one* very strong feeling: *this* was what she wanted to do in the future; she wanted to become a doctor and do surgery!

'I want to learn how to do surgery too!' she said to her father when they were on the way back home. He was silent at first and looked at her from the side with twinkling eyes.

'That won't be possible, child. With your middle school

exam record you won't be able to become a doctor, but you can become a nurse. A surgery-nurse maybe.'

'No!' she yelled angrily. 'I want to do it myself – and not stand next to it!'

He could have said: 'You should've been less lazy and done your best like your sister.' But he was not like that; he probably did not even think something like that. He said:

'Then you must keep studying after middle school; that must be possible. First the high school and after that, university. I'll ask the doctor how we should go about it....'

She did not like to study at all. Her sister, with all her grade nines, was already going to the high school in the city – she went to the girls' middle school close to home, and she did it reluctantly. But from that day on, something pushed her forwards that was stronger than her laziness.

I see you in a thousand images
Maria, sweetly expressed,
But none of them could paint you
As my soul glimpses you.

Novalis (1772-1801)

Almost all Catholic girls are called Maria, although they are not called by that name. She, the younger of the two sisters, *was* called Maria. You felt your name as the external shape of your being, from your true being. Shy as she was, this shyness became much stronger when someone approached her with her name. You had the feeling that someone took off your coat and placed you in the full daylight. She did not like it at all to stand out and on hearing her name, the blush of shame would rise to her cheeks. Maria... she shared her name with the most blessed among women; what else could you do but be ashamed when someone called *you* with that name? Inside herself, hidden very deep, she carried a presumption... a desire to truly be Maria. But if that longing became a little conscious... she was even more ashamed. She was afraid of her own haughtiness....

She studied better than her sister, but was never complimented for it extensively. Her parents thought that intelligence was a good thing, but not really important. It is about love, about sacrifice, about attention and interest in your fellow man. If intelligence can contribute to that, it is beautiful. However, on its *own* it is not worth so much.

23

This was how her mother and father lived and although they would never openly state this view, the whole farm with its farmyard and orchard emanated their attitude to life.

She liked reading a lot and in the winter she could sit near the stove for hours with a book from the library. In the summer she had her place on the border of the farmyard, in the sun, then away from the sun. She liked stories about holy men and novels about knights. Children's books did not interest her much. While reading, she felt how she was taken into a world that she missed and which she longed for with a growing sadness.

Studying was her other hobby. She wanted to go forward and always had a look at the last pages of the ready reckoner to see if she was already able to do the sums. Her sister thought she was a show-off, but she was not. She strove for knowledge, only for *learning*, for enrichment, for development of her abilities. She did not get full marks for geography because she found it so important to *know* where everything 'was' – she experienced *how* one could learn something like that. She had never travelled further than Heerlen and Maastricht, so a city like Amsterdam only spoke to her through pictures and stories. That was how you discovered how you could remember in images and also in words. In images everything was a lot richer, but it also took more time to study in that way. In words, it went fast, but she became exhausted. One did not have to *learn* how to calculate, you had to *be able* to do it by understanding it. Language was done by means of her *sense* for it and completed by means of several rules. So she actually played with studying, while her sister did monkey tricks and did not feel like making even a little effort.

She went to the high school in the city. There she discovered how *alone* she was in her effort. Of course there were a lot of intelligent girls who got the best grades like her. But she did not find them to be interested in studying *itself*, which was just the case with her. Because of her timidity, she stood back and moreover, she felt ill at her ease as a farmer's daughter between the daughters of doctors, notaries and rich business people. But one girl continuously sought her company. Maria was always astonished how easily the friendship arose with this beautiful, easygoing, rich girl from the city. Every time she felt lonely, she found her friend beside her, at the school-desk, on her bike, in gym class, at the school party.

'Will you come to our house to sleep over some time? Friday? Will you come after school and stay with us!'

She was stepping into a different world....

The house was in a villa quarter of the city, with a big garden. Here there was no disorganized farmyard with old chairs against a wall in the sun and her father dressed in an overall, wearing wooden shoes. Here, every blade of grass seemed cultivated; the tiles around the sea-blue swimming pool were polished and shiny, the bushes cut in shape. At home, the roses blossomed untamed around the gate out to the grass-land – here, the gardener determined how far they could grow. The father was a man at a distance. In his work as a notary he dressed like her father did for a funeral…. She saw the mother only in the evening; she had a busy job. She was a distinguished lady in a suit, her arms and fingers decorated with gold and diamonds.

'On Friday evening we always eat rolls and soup.' she said apologizing. 'I hope you don't mind.'

Later she sat quietly at the table. The parents were talking; she took everything in intensely. She was used to talking in the Limburg dialect at home; here, they spoke Dutch. The father was a real gentleman, who spoke solemnly, as if he was reading a will. From time to time he looked at her inquiringly through his glasses. After dinner they sat at the table and the father directed himself to her.

'Tell me, Maria, how do you like it here at school?'

A sort of force came right through her warm shyness. Blushing, she looked at the gentleman and answered:

'It's nice, but I do have to get used to it….'

'I hear that you get such good grades. Do you study a lot?'

'I don't have to study so much, sir. If you pay attention at school, you don't have to study so much afterwards.'

'Most children don't pay much attention.' he said, smiling. 'Do you find it so interesting?'

'Not always. I think the lessons are interesting, they're all different. I mostly pay attention to that and then I also listen to what they're saying.'

'Can we leave the table?!!' the two brothers yelled impatiently. The father made a consenting move, and asked

Maria further:

'And what would you like to do in the future?'

Was this question just asked out of politeness, or was this gentleman really interested.... she did not know. She shrugged her shoulders lightly and said:

'I have no idea. I only know the orchard and the bakery and so on. And the school. I don't know yet what I can become.

'A girl like you must make the right decision. Think about it well!'

She felt sympathy from him. He liked her and made that clear to her.

'Can we finally do something else now, dad?'

That someone dared to ask a gentleman like that such a thing! Father nodded and said:

'You should come here often, child. I would enjoy talking to you again.'

They watched TV the whole night. She was delighted, because they did not have one at home yet. She watched the news, and after that, a quiz and then a movie. In bed they chatted deep into the night, and the morning did not start before eleven....

'Are we also allowed to swim?' she asked after breakfast.

She had been wondering for a little while if one could ask something like that – and finally mustered the courage. She enjoyed the fresh water and drying off in the sun, and the tea with gooseberry cake that the mother brought them. When she came home late in the afternoon at last, she felt confused. She suddenly saw the old farm, the muddy farmyard, the broken chairs, the dog, the chickens and the rabbits in a completely different light. Everything was in bad repair, but clean. Her parents walked around in old clothes – but clean. Did she feel dissatisfaction? Her mother cut thick slices of grey and black bread; on a dish was a chunk of butter, the table was set with a plastic cover and with pottery from which fragments were missing. It smelled like manure, green soap and animals.... Grandpa was smoking his pipe and spread his own scent. She quietly sat at the table and prayed along with the Lord's Prayer.

'And, Maria?' her father asked. 'How was it at the notary's house?'

'Good. But also strange, a little weird. I don't know. Everything is very beautiful and stylish; they have a whole room full of books and records, there're paintings on the walls and thick carpets on the floor. They were all very nice and the father... was mainly nice. Do you understand, daddy?'

His blue eyes smiled a little sadly. He nodded.

'Such a gentleman has something that we cannot offer. He has studied and knows a lot. Such people live very differently, Maria.'

'Don't they live good lives, then?'

'Different.... We have our garden and we have our faith – and we have each other. There is no more, and we don't need more. But you, Maria... are gifted and you will outgrow all this here...'

'That's not true, daddy! Never!'

'Yes, child. I don't mean that you'll reject us, but you'll discover a different world. A world that we here do not know, but which is open to you. Set off, child. Talents must be used, you know that. Discover as much as you can – we are behind you.'

Why did she have to cry a little bit? Was daddy sad? He got up and took the crying child into his arms. From that day on, she set off....

'Why are people on earth? What do you think, child?'

The notary often asked her questions like that, when they were sitting at the table a little longer after dinner. She got used to his direct approach; however, she never saw that he spoke to his daughter or wife like that.

Why are we on earth...? There was a standard answer to that question in the catechism. She shivered and said:

'In order to love, I think. To learn to love. I want to become like my father....'

'So what is your father like, then?'

'She reflected on that. She knew what he was like through and through but did not have the words for it.

'He works and observes. And he prays. My father is like that.

'He observes?'

'I mean – not only with his eyes. He looks and listens and understands, everything always very calmly, without comment. He lets you be completely free; he just observes. He doesn't interfere, ever. It isn't necessary, because you can't do otherwise in his presence than be in complete agreement with him.'

She saw astonishment in the grey eyes behind the glasses. She was young to be so bright, she knew that. Maybe too bright. But the notary liked that and he stimulated her to think and speak her mind.

'And you would like to be like that too?'

She thought about the other world that was now added to her trusted one, the world of this intelligent man opposite her. The world that she got to know at school. That was not her father's quality; he did not need that. She shivered again and said shyly:

'Yes. But I also want more....' She lowered her eyes, because otherwise she could not express that 'more'. 'I also want to be... like you. I want to *know* more than my father. I have more questions than he has. But still one would become less from that than he is. Knowing seems like a kind of sin, as if it makes you less *good*, or something.'

'Is he against your going to grammar school, girl?'

Clearly the notary did not understand her. She answered:

'He's never against anything; that's the whole point. He only observes.'

'He must have his opinions? For example, that you must go to church on Sunday?'

She shook her head intensely.

'He goes and because we're his children we must go too. But other people don't have to go; they have to understand that for themselves.'

'Of course. But he surely doesn't agree if they don't.'

'For him it's neither good nor bad. You should see his eyes. He looks very thoughtful, but doesn't judge.'

And you? What do you think?'

'I think the same. Other people have the right to choose for themselves what's right and what's wrong.'

'What sense does it make to know a lot, to be intelligent?'

'I don't know. I don't think it makes sense to know a lot, but the studying does, being busy with it.'

He smiled.

'So all those thick books that I have studied – it all makes no sense?'

She did not like conflict in conversation, and she also had great respect for the notary. But she had to explain what she meant.

'Of course it's necessary, but it doesn't make sense.'

'You mean: when you are dead, everything is gone.'

She nodded.

'Yes, I believe that's what I mean. What my father does isn't gone then, but *knowledge* is. I think so, I feel it's like that.'

'And still you want to know more?'

She became sad and only nodded.

'You have to stop, Bas. The child's getting upset,' the mother said, a little angry.

'Be quiet,' the notary said, and to Maria: 'I don't want to hurt you, girl. I'm just interested. You're an intelligent girl and very deep. I don't come across someone like that often. It's a miracle how different people are and how different their ideals. You have much potential, and I'd like to stimulate it a little.'

'I don't mind,' she said softly.

He got up and tapped her cheek in a friendly way. The gesture touched her deeply....

'My father is acting very stupidly!' Roos said. 'Come on,

let's watch TV.'

Maria acted like she was interested in the TV, but she was very touched and could not release herself from her feelings.

She felt a great respect for the notary and experienced his loneliness. All people are alone... they have their deep strivings and longings. But she was also a little scared of him. He made her feel that he was a *man*, and she a girl....

She wanted to talk about it with her father, but she did not know how. She did not know if it belonged to his world.

She looked for him by his fruit trees and as always, he immediately stopped working.

'So child. How was it at Roos's?'

He always saw exactly how things were with her....

'Nice. But that father, dad....'

He sat with her on the tree stump, close to her. She felt him, his body, but mainly *him*.

'What's wrong with that father?'

'Roos tells me that he's much nicer to me than he is to her. She always argues with him, but when I'm around he's full of interest and asks me all kinds of questions.'

Her father put his hand on her knee.

'You're not a child anymore, Maria. You're fifteen years old and becoming a beautiful girl – '

'Agnes is much prettier.'

'A beautiful girl you are. Innocent, busy as a bee and willing. Every man looks for a noble woman – but finds after marriage that he has a woman who manages the money and has a comment about everything.'

'And what about mom?'

'Mom is my companion. But my noble woman is the Stella Maris[1]… the Mother of God. Nevertheless, a man looks for the noble woman in his girlfriend, his wife.'

What did he mean? That the notary was in love with her? She shivered. He put his arm around her.

'You've been a believing child and now you're slowly turning into a grown-up woman. Your being *touches* the notary, Maria. Don't be afraid! Never be afraid to *touch* people.'

She sighed.

'I'm not afraid, daddy. He touches me too, because he calls on something in me every time. The things we learn at school are making it hard for me to keep believing. What we have to believe is contradictory to science. And it's actually not possible; miracles never happen anymore now. Who says that it was like that then? A human being could never die and rise again?'

'Not a human being, Maria. Not a human being, but a God. That makes the Christian faith so completely different from all other religions. We don't believe in a dogma, we believe in a *deed,* a *deed* of God in a human body. That *that* is a mystery I will not want to deny. But your father, Maria – I've kept my whole life going by that mystery. Later on, there will be fruit on our trees here and after that, they become motionless, the trees. As silent as death. An apparently dead tree keeps standing. Isn't it a miracle that

---

[1]   In Maastricht is a little chapel with Maria. She is being worshipped there as Maria, Sterre der Zee, Star of the sea…

from this wood in spring the buds sprout again? Miracles? They happen everyday. Every day, Maria! The interest of the notary for a simple girl like you - is a miracle!'

'But the mystery you spoke about, the centre of our faith, goes much further. That isn't to be compared to a real, completely dead tree which buds sprout from anyway. That's really not possible. But still we have to believe that, nothing less than that!'

Father said seriously:

'The words 'believe' and 'must' are not compatible with each other, child. Faith unites with the full, unrestrained will. I'll tell you once again: to your father there is no question about faith in a dogma. It's faith in a deed and that deed lives on in our time. There're chosen ones who can observe that He is still among us. That observation works through in all the details of ordinary life, Maria.'

In this patient way he demonstrated carefully to her the origin of his peace, his devotion, his observation. She knew now that he, her father, had observed Him. She knew now why she wanted to become like him.

When she finished her exams, the notary came to the farm with his wife to drink a cup of coffee along with a piece of cake. She was very nervous, but her mother took away all her nervousness with her cheerful talk. She baked a whole worktop full of cakes, and the smell of freshly-baked pastry and strong coffee put everyone in an expectant mood. The front room was aired and polished for the occasion, and the man sat down there immediately, while mother captivated the notary's wife by showing her the kitchen and outbuildings with the enormous stock of preserved fruits and vegetables. Maria and Roos cut the pastry in big wedges, while Agnes whipped the cream using two forks. Agnes was a little edgy, because her sister had already finished her finals, while she still had to go to school for two more years. Besides, she did not like it that her sister was the centre of attention; she was not used to that!

Maria was always 'inside' her sister with half of her feelings, so she did not fail to notice how Agnes felt.

'Shall I help you?' she asked warmly.

'No, never mind. It's your party,' grumbled Agnes.

Maria shrugged her shoulders and thought about the two men in the front room. How would it go? They knew each other from the stories that she, Maria, told. Now they had actually met each other...

They smoked an expensive cigar together and talked about the council elections. She could not believe it! Now they were finally together, at her party, and what were they doing? Talking about something as external as politics!

She carried in the tray with cups of coffee on it and presented the coffee to both men. Agnes came in with the cake, followed by the two mothers.

'Can I put the radio on?' Agnes asked cheekily, and put the music on.

'They're two different characters!' the notary said meaningfully. 'We've had Maria with us with pleasure and shall miss her now she's going to college so far away. I've tried for years to induce her to study law and at first she rather liked the idea. But step by step, it became clear after all that she has a calling for the most beautiful of the professions:

to be a doctor!'

Agnes looked bitter. Maria had only imitated her – and now she had even started her studies earlier!

'I don't know if it's a calling,' Maria said, blushing. 'I also wanted to go into a convent, but I don't dare to take that big step. You don't really know what you're getting into, and it's a definite choice, like marriage. I'd feel committed to be faithful to that choice.'

'It's a huge difference. Studying for the spirit or living for the body, for health.' The notary turned to her father. 'Don't you think so?'

'In the end they're not so different. I can say: "I live for nature" and "I live for the spirit" and they're equally right.'

'Those are two different sides in a man. They're not active at the same time. You work in the country or you pray.'

Father shook his head carefully.

'To me working in the countryside is always an act of prayer. You could also be a doctor like that.'

'And a notary?' asked the notary, smiling.

'Also a notary. Although, you work on the threshold between body and spirit, do you not?'

'You have given this quite some thought,' the notary concluded.

'Ah, no... it's all obvious to me. Let's not talk about me. Maria is on the threshold of life in the great world. That's a special moment.'

'Maria is a very clever girl. She will study rightly and live sensibly.'

'She must also be a *student*. Seeing what's going on in the big city, going out, making friends.'

'Why did you pick Amsterdam?'

'She chose it. We've never been there, but the capital attracts her the most.'

She sat there uncomfortably. It was not so simple…. She wanted to study medicine from a longing for truth in the study, and Amsterdam… sounded a lot better than Nijmegen, or Utrecht. It was far away and she dreaded to leave her home. She would only be able to travel home now and then; the train trip was too expensive. She would miss her parents, she would even miss Agnes; however, she also looked forward to being her own boss. Agnes always wanted to decide everything….

When the notary had left, a deep sadness came into her heart. Ah, she would visit them often, the farewell was not for ever. But everything *did* become completely different. Roos failed her exams; she had to stay at school another year and would take home other friends, who would sit with her at the table and to whom her father would direct his questions.

*

In two separate worlds with a common environment: this is how the two girls lived. Agnes could be extremely annoyed by her sister. She thought that she was slow and boring – but she could not ignore her. If Maria went her own way, as in her friendship with that notary's daughter, she was extremely jealous. She could not stand that Roos, that beautiful doll! But when she had to take Maria

37

along when she wanted to go out with Jet, she was fed up with her well-behaved sister. She was zealous, submissive and devout. Agnes herself hated being active; she tried to escape from every assignment and in church she was always counting the minutes.

'If daddy weren't so very strict, I wouldn't go on Sundays,' she complained to Maria.

'You're crazy! He allows you *everything*!'

'Not at all! When you have such a father, you *can't* do what you want. You wouldn't be able to face him anymore. You can't do that to him.'

'Then you *shouldn't* say that he is strict! It's inside you, *you* can't resist him, even if you wanted to.'

'Jet can do anything...'

'If her parents find out what she 'does', she will be beaten.'

'A beating's soon over. *We* must always be good, because daddy's so nice and mommy so cheerful.'

'Who'd complain about happiness! You must be really crazy. So you'd rather have a beating?'

'Yes, said Agnes fiercely. Maria and daddy... they were the same. You couldn't do anything about it because they were always nice and honest. Still, she played tricks and then Maria had to tell lies with her. She would never betray her but she did blame Agnes. It never came out, because daddy was very trusting, which also worked humiliating again. Moreover, you had the feeling that he understood anyway and just allowed it. Anyway, all that goodness made Agnes sick. She thought her family was boring and superficial - uninformed about what's for sale in the world.

Limburg girls walked around in skirts and dresses at that time. Trousers were only allowed in cold winters, but then you had to wear a skirt on top of them, which of course looked hideous. Agnes wanted to have one of those pairs of jeans, like the ones you could buy in the big city. She stole a guilder from her mother's purse every week that was always on a shelf in the kitchen. After half a year she could buy a pair, in a roundabout way. She hid them at Jet's and only put them on when they were together, with the boys. Even Maria could not know. You had to lie down on the floor to get them closed, they were so tight. Then you suddenly felt your behind... If she was wearing them, she provoked the boys, who she did not allow to do anything, of course. She tempted them and rejected them again. It was the best game yet.

At school she did not do anything, not even when she knew that she wanted to become a surgeon. Her father made it possible for her, through the doctor, that she was allowed to go to high school after middle school. But she had to go back two classes. So she went to the same college as Maria, who was two classes higher at the Gymnasium (high school). If only *she* were in Maria's place! Oh, she would have exploited her lead! She would have cold-shouldered her sister! But not Maria... she was nice to her, showed her around everywhere and so on. She was not even happy with that. Maria was a bitch! A sister to be ashamed of!

*

Everyone, really everyone, lives from a deep intense longing. As Novalis says, desire is the most beautiful gift that the soul has received. It makes man *strive* and that striving is unlimited. As a child that longing at first comes to expression in giving shape to the body as perfectly as possible and it is clear that this can only happen from the deepest unconscious part of us.

Were the mind to help only a little in that, the body would become a ruin. For the mind is much too small, too limited, to be able to accomplish such a great thing. Later this longing expresses itself – it is still objective – in the ability to *learn*. But then, with puberty, the time comes when that longing starts to live in the consciousness, not fully, but as a deep enthusiasm that now takes on a subjective character. Please do not think that it is a matter of *any* genetic ability here, or of environment influences. Those determine only the *shape* that the longing takes on, never the individual character of it. That individual character comes from far distances of time, from levels of human being inaccessible to the mind.

The soul can be so pure and permeable that the original, objective desire, which is of a purely spiritual nature, takes shape undistorted in life. In the inner life there are no limits, and the force is so great that the external circumstances – genes and environment – can be applied to the best advantage...

But the soul can also be filled with lust for itself. Then, the original longing is weakened. Hereditary tendencies and surroundings assume the upper hand then, or can even be employed...

*

The developing girl Agnes was moved by a burning fire of desire. She was beautiful, always in love with herself and keen to prove herself in all aspects of life, but without having to do too much to achieve it. She wanted to be the best, but it had to be effortless. She also wanted to be the most beautiful, for which she did at least make the effort of putting on red lipstick and black eyeliner. She loved to show herself off and keenly looked out for chances to do so. It was no problem for her to tell lies in order to do that.… She would sleep over at a friend's house on Friday evenings, but nobody knew that her friend was a girl of twenty years old, who already had a car and with whom she went into the city to dance until the middle of the night at the bar that stayed open longest.… If necessary, they drove across the border to Belgium or Germany. They danced with soldiers from the barracks. With a lust in herself she dove deep into her awakening soul and its powerful life of desire…

She got herself the Pill from a doctor who lived far from home and she rewarded a soldier now and then who was very generous or just very handsome. When they asked her how old she was, she was always eighteen or even twenty. Every Friday night she was twenty…

At the middle school there were problems. She was intelligent enough, but she could not bring out that little extra bit of attention. Her thoughts were everywhere, except at

41

school. In the fourth grade she was kept back for a year.

'Agnes, we have to talk seriously,' said her father. 'It seems better to me that you just get a job. You have your middle school diploma, you can become a waitress or a typist, or you can work with us at the farm. What's going on now doesn't make sense. You'll be twenty when you pass your exam - if you get it then. We shouldn't want something that isn't there.'

Feeling deeply insulted, she said:

'It *is* there. I can do it.'

'I don't doubt that, child. You only lack the *will*. If you want to become a surgeon, a wish and a talent is not enough. You must also *want* it.'

'I do want it!'

'You want it a lot, but you don't apply yourself. Effort is will. You don't have enough *will*.'

She was deeply, deeply offended. And also a little desperate. Her father was really not crazy, even though he always remained friendly. If he stopped supporting her, she could forget it. Then she would have to be inferior for the rest of her life, at first to a boss, later to a husband. She sat up straight and looked at her father.

'Let me stay at school for one more year, dad. Please? I'll show you that I do have *will*. And if I do move over to the next grade with high marks, you'll allow me to finish school. Yes? Please?'

She was good at charming people to get her way, but with her father that was not even necessary. He simply looked straight back at her and said calmly:

'All right, Agnes. That's a deal.' He stuck out his hand and grabbed her strongly. 'Show me what you can do.'

She was too proud to give in to her laziness; she still left her homework, but at school she paid attention well and for one test she even studied for an hour. She came home with A's and B's....

When she was twenty she passed her finals with flying colours. Now there was no notary and his wife and daughter, but a lot of friends and girlfriends, the whole family, farmer Erens and his wife with all their kids in tow – and Maria from Amsterdam.

They ate and drank until midnight. Agnes had passed her exams!

Where is the truth?
In the tangible object as
In a mirror.
In the reason in the way of
Arguing and speaking,
In the intellect in the way of
Assumptions and results,
In the Spirit in the actual and
Living form.

Giordano Bruno (1548-1600)

The world into which Maria entered turned out to be larger than she ever expected. Of course at home she had looked at the evening sky covered with stars with great respect and felt how *huge* the world was, how endlessly huge. Amsterdam was big in a different way. The houses were enormously high, the number of streets with such houses seemed countless. The streets were so busy and there were different languages to be heard. At home she had been able to fill the world with her *being*; here she felt modest and unpretentious, and above all, lonely. Foreign in a world that seemed to be familiar to everyone and in which everyone seemed to know each other – except her. She knew nobody and nobody knew her.

Nevertheless, it was not hard for her to fall in love with the city. She took lonely walks along the city's canals, admired the house fronts and enjoyed in silence the emergence of the autumn colours. She had little money to spend, but she loved to look around in the 'Bijenkorf' without buying anything. There was something special about this city… a certain 'aroma', which she had not observed anywhere else.

She could not become a member of a sorority; she had

no money for that. But when the colleges had started, she did engage in conversations now and then. She felt lost between the hundreds of novices, but she always sat between one or two others, they were close enough to chat with. Soon there was a boy who sought her company. She had no interest in boys, they did not arouse anything in her… and yet, like all girls, she longed to have a boyfriend. This boy could not be considered at all. She thought he was unattractive, sloppily dressed, his hair was unwashed, in the breaks a handrolled cigarette was hanging between his lips…. His fingers were yellow… and that voice! A complaining, unsatisfied sound it was; he criticized everyone and everything.

'Where do you come from?' he asked her.

'South Limburg, a little south of Heerlen. And you?'

'Amsterdam. I am a real Amsterdammer.' It sounded proud. She had nothing more to say. He did.

'Why did you come to Amsterdam?'

She felt that he expected a good motivation and answered stubbornly:

'Because. It seemed nice.'

'Have you ever been here before?'

'No.'

She wanted to get rid of him; on the other hand, she was happy that she was not standing there alone….

'Do you know any people here?'

'No.'

'What's your name?'

'Maria.'

'My Gosh! My name's René.'

'Why My Gosh?'

'It sounds kind of – er... religious.'

'So?'

She felt she had rejected him, but he evidently rather liked that and just kept talking.

'Do you believe in Maria?'

'Yes.'

'Dear God! It's good that you came to Amsterdam; you can wake up here from your dreams.'

'What do you have to do with my dreams?'

College started again and she felt him creepily close to her. She smelled the dirty tobacco smell and the greasy hair and shivered.

In the afternoon he asked:

'Will you come with me for a sandwich?'

'I have no money. I've got my lunch with me.'

'Then I'll buy you a coffee, or tea. Yes?'

Everything better than being alone again, at least he was a human being, to whom she could talk. At a table in a café they had a coffee. She could not help inhaling thick clouds of smoke. She asked:

'You must know a lot of people here?'

He looked bitter and said:

'They all think that they've made it.'

She shrugged her shoulders. What of it? Actually she felt pity for him, so full of hatred against everything around him. His antipathy summoned up hers, and so he was totally alone.

'I have tickets for a concert,' he said casually. 'Do you want to come?'

'What kind of concert?' She had never been to a concert before.

'Chamber music in the small hall of the Concertgebouw.'

'How did you come by them?'

'I play cello.'

She did not even really know what a cello was... a stringed instrument? In any case, the cello put him in a different light.

'Do you like it? Are you good at it?'

'Yes. Two times yes. I could've gone to the Con., but I wanted to become a doctor after all.'

'The Con.?'

'The Conservatory. Where you get educated to be a performing musician.'

Because she thought he was so unattractive, her foolishness did not harm her. She truly did not care what he thought of her; he did not have to come looking for her all the time.

'So? Will you come with me?'

'I don't have any money. Really.'

'They're already paid for, by my parents.'

'All right. When?'

'Friday night.'

They saw each other at the entrance. She had never been in this neighbourhood before; she lived in a small room in one of those endless streets in Amsterdam-West. He was already there. Strange, that someone that was so antipathetic could nevertheless become sympathetic towards you. She immediately noticed that he had washed his hair and was wearing a white shirt and a jacket that was too large for him above his worn trousers. She saw his happiness when he spotted her.

'Hey, Maria! This is our concert hall.'

He directed her inside, put up her coat and bought her a soda. In the wall mirror she saw how they stood there. A tall girl with blond hair in a ponytail, with a common face and dressed in an old-fashioned dress and a drip of a boy in tatty clothes, but they looked nice somehow.

They went into a small hall with dark red chairs. She only knew something like that from TV. She enjoyed the authenticity of it all. A real concert hall and later on, live musicians. She sat next to him and felt really happy. Not with his closeness, but with the life in which he apparently was at home. With the city, the full hall, the brilliant lighting, the red plush seats... although they were very worn. She had a feeling of expectation, of astonishment. She did not know classical music; at home there was no music, except sometimes the radio. What would it be like?

Two women and two men in black took their places on stage.

'That's a cello!' René pointed at the man with the largest instrument.

They tuned, and everyone in the hall became as quiet as mice. The musicians started together.

Was it possible to listen to each tone separately and at the same time together? She felt overwhelmed by the abundance of impressions that came together in such harmonious confusion. She knew nothing about music, but here a shocking love was born.

'This was not actually written for a string quartet.' René gave her a lesson in music in the break. 'Bach was the great exponent of the fugue and he composed this work on the letters of his own name B.A.C.H.'

She did not understand a word of what he said and only saw his enthusiasm. Here the hatred that had seemed so inherent in him was completely gone.

'What did you think of it?' he asked at last.

'I don't know...' she stammered.

'You didn't like it at all,' he decided.

'Really I did. So much so that I don't know what to say. I'm overwhelmed that such a thing exists....'

'Are we going for a drink?' he asked afterwards.

'No, I want to go home,' she said, avoiding the invitation. 'I'm tired and tomorrow my sister's coming to sleep over. I'll have to show her the city and she'll want all kinds of things that I don't.'

He also wanted a lot of things that she did not want; she felt it only too well. He said:

'You're so naïve, Maria. I think that's sweet...' and he walked away.

They became the best of friends. She knew that he was in love with her, and he knew that his love remained unrequited. He chose friendship, and she accepted it thankfully. Through him she quickly got to know and love Amsterdam. He asked her over to his home, for a cup of tea....

He lived with his parents in a maisonette near the concert hall. His mother was a violinist, his father a sculptor. He was their only child. While she cycled to his house she thought of her parental home. The farm with the swept farmyard, the carefully maintained vegetable and flower garden, the orchard... the scrubbed tile floors inside and the old wood in beeswax. She could only go home once every six weeks; there was no money to go more often. Now she cycled to René, who still lived with his parents. She rang the doorbell, and the door was pulled open. She was standing at the bottom of a long, steep flight of stairs.

'Come on up!' René called.

She jumped up the stairs, but at the same time observed how *dirty* the stairs were. Hair, dust, and grease spots everywhere. The maisonette was beautifully light, but just as dirty everywhere. It smelled like cat piss, old coffee and alcohol with cigar smoke. The windows were so dirty that you could hardly look outside, the wooden floor was full of cat hairs and was sticky with dirt. She hardly dared to breathe, as if the air was poisoned with all the smells of old food....

'Sorry for the mess. But you must be used to a lot yourself at the farm. This is my mother.'

A tall woman with a benign glance inspected her from head to foot. She wore her grey-blond hair in a bun, and wore an old T-shirt with a long flowing skirt, in lilac and purple tints. She held out her hand and said:

'Hello, Maria. Do you want a cup of tea? Black or herbal tea?'

She did not know the difference but 'black' did not sound appealing, so she said:

'Hello, madam. Herbal tea please.'

'Do sit down.'

But where? On the couch and the chairs cats were dozing. René cleared a chair for her. She sat down and looked around. What she thought was beautiful was the filtered city light and the wall covered with books.

'Your parents read a lot?' she asked.

'They have spiritual interests. That's not in my line, by the way.'

Spiritual....? She asked:

'What's the difference between spiritual and religious?'

'They think that they can gain knowledge about the spirit that lives in the world. You Catholic people deny that and think of it as something impossible, as an enormous conceit.'

'And what about you?'

'I only know my own world, Maria, like I see it. That's my reality. I don't know yet if I can see something more in it than nature; now I see nothing more than nature and human creations. The only thing you really know is yourself; for the rest you don't know if what you think of it is correct or not.'

'I just think that one knows everything better than oneself, René! One has no objectivity about oneself, unlike with everything else.'

'What is the use of objectivity, if I can't enter that 'other'? Do I know what you think, feel, want? That's impossible, right? But myself I really know!'

She shut up. It was just a matter of consideration. His mother entered with the tea.

'Make some room on the table, René.'

René took away some dirty glasses, so the tray fitted on the table. The tea was in a glass pot with old scale at the bottom.

'How do you like Amsterdam?' she asked. The question was a formality, convention.

Maria's answer was too: 'Nice,' she said.

'Now, I'll leave you to it. I have to teach.'

She whirled out of the room. René put on some music.

'Okay...Otherwise we'll only hear the screeching of beginner violinists. Terrible.'

She had the feeling that all her self-confidence, her common sociability, her joy of life drained away here. There was only a small stream of insecurity left. She wanted to get out of here!

'Do you never think about leaving your parents' house and living by yourself, René?'

'I'm very well off here, and it's free. I can do whatever I want.'

'But it's very different, being away from home. It's more than looking after yourself and being able to do whatever you want.'

She was relieved that she could go after an hour. On her bike she allowed her thoughts and feelings into her heart. Abomination... and pity for René. It was inhospitable there, like a rose-tree eaten bare by rabbits. No warmth, no care, no understanding. Nothing. Spirituality?

*

53

When she was a second-year student she fell in love for the first time. In love, like a twelve year-old girl…. She kept her feelings secret, looked for no approach at all, but adored the young idol from a safe distance. It was a boy who assisted with the physiology practical. He was tall and well-built, had a beautiful head with blond hair and blue eyes. Those eyes were so blue that you almost could not look into them. An unlikely blue and always smiling. In every respect he was the opposite of her friend René, with whom she hung around as with a brother. This young man wore his white lab coat impeccably, was dressed casually, and usually he was… optimistic and positive. Whenever she entered the laboratory she first looked around to see if he was there. He always was. Then the afternoon was like a party for her. But halfway through, after the tea break, the pain of the approaching parting already started again. It always became five o'clock, and then she had to leave and bear the searing pain in her soul that lasted until the next afternoon. She never talked to him, maybe he did not even see her. But to her he became the example of a *man*. If she would ever get married, it would be to such a man, or else she would not get married at all. She looked for the *sun*, the smile, the trust, the light, the warmth….

The last day of the practical she knew it would be a parting for ever. She would never see him again. He was already busy with his doctorate and you never ran into senior students. When the afternoon started, an eternity of being together seemed to lie before her, but every second took something away from that – and at last it became five o'clock, the time of death… the absolute good-bye.

When she left the laboratory she looked at him and for a moment his glance met hers. He gave her a friendly smile and said:

'Good luck with your studies.'

She nodded and went outside.

It started to get dark and it was hailing.

She put up her collar and ran to the cycle shed. Ahead of her there seemed to be fifty years of loneliness…

*

Of course, Agnes also went to Amsterdam. She had already been at Maria's several times and had enjoyed going out on the Leidseplein and the streets around it. But there would always be the drag of her sister: 'Come home with me now! You can't go with such a stranger! I don't feel like staying anymore, I don't like this at all!' She would have to water the wine, although she preferred to drink it *undiluted*. Now she had finally come so far. But the city was very big, and here a girl from Limburg meant nothing, even if she was very beautiful like her…. She was one of the many students and after a few days she was happy that she 'had' the company of Maria and that weird friend of hers, René. They were already third year students, they knew the city and the people, the right and the wrong places… they had a group of friends and Agnes was taken in immediately.

' Are you dating that guy René, or not?' she asked Maria.

They were together at Maria's dining table. She had a bigger room now, in a students' house in Zuid (South).

Maria was beautiful, after all, and so independent. She accomplished a lot here in Amsterdam. She still wore her hair in a ponytail, but it was a little looser than before. Her blue eyes looked sweet and sensible, like she naturally *was*. Agnes felt like a wild gipsy compared to her noble sister. But she would never, *never* want to be like Maria. Maria looked at her and said:

'What René and I have is friendship. I tried to escape from it, because he did not attract me at all, and he fell in love with me – and that remains the same. But he wants to stay friends and he truly *is* a friend.'

'I think that's *sad*!' Agnes cried out. 'Do you know how *terrible* it is to have to deal with unrequited love?'

'What would you want, then? That I start something with someone I dislike?'

'I've done that so many times. It can become rather nice!'

Maria shivered.

'I've only been attracted to a boy once, physically as well as mentally. That's the way it should be for me, nothing else!'

'You are so thorough! What do you actually think of your studies?'

Maria shrugged her shoulders:

'When you have experienced *authenticity* in your youth, everything disappoints you later on. I think it's a sort of blank science, human knowledge without the human being. I can only study with indifference, because it has to be done.'

'Why *has to be done*?'

'You have to do something, right? This still seems the best

to me. But I can't *experience* anything with it.'

' You don't have to. You just learn a *profession*.'

'René has the same problem as I do. Only he solves it with constant grumbling about everything. That doesn't help him at all; it only makes him grumpy.'

'A strange guy. Why doesn't he dress better? Why don't you say anything about it?'

'I have nothing to do with that, do I? You should tell him. That would be so much like you!'

Once college and practical lessons started, she made friends easily. She had great charisma and she *knew* it. She also felt that she was in the right place in her medical studies. For the first time the subject matter did not bore her, and she really wanted to achieve something. There was a world of possibilities before her.... she would become a doctor and gain status.... and wealth. She would be a woman who gave shape to her own life, with great energy and merciless if she had to be. No, she never wanted to become like Maria, so boring and quiet. She wouldn't accomplish anything, even if she became a doctor. Her sister didn't understand anything about life. Nevertheless, she liked being around her, because she was sweet. She was like daddy, with his understanding for everything and everyone. If you had a problem – and that happened often – you could go to her. She listened and valued you. She did not give unasked-for advice, but she did give the right advice. It was only when one wanted to have fun that one should not come to her, because she preferred seriousness....

One night, she met René at her sister's. They were eating together and Maria instantly put another plate on the table.

'Join us, Agnes. There is enough for three.'

There was classical music on, and the room was cosily lighted. Agnes felt comfortable. René always cast admiring eyes on her, even though he had already been in love with Maria for more than two years.

'How can twin sisters be so different?' René sighed.

'That's a cliché. We've heard that already a thousand times,' Agnes said snappily.

'What do you actually have in common?' René asked imperturbably.

'A common past. And we complement each other well. We know how the other feels, even if we don't talk. We're like best friends, but it's uncomplicated, because of the blood-tie.'

'Do you live in exactly the same world then? Do you agree with each other? Do you have the same interests?'

'Not at all.'

'That seems nice...' René said, absorbed in thought. 'Two individuals in one internal world.'

'All individuals have one common internal world,' Maria said. 'That it seems to be different is because of the difference in experience.'

'That's your view, I know that.' René said. 'I don't see it like that. I live *alone* in my internal world, completely alone.'

'That's because of your strong feelings of withdrawal. If you had more sympathy, you wouldn't be lonely.'

Agnes looked at the two of them. Maria was educating the boy, it seemed. He looked up to her enormously... she was his great example. She suddenly understood something about René. Maria was not really accessible; she was too high above them. Agnes did not need all that fighting and searching; to her the purpose of life was clear. She got up.

'I'm leaving. It was pleasant.'

René got also up hastily.

'I'll cycle with you.'

He put on his worn jacket, put up his collar and caressed Maria's hair.

'Bye, beautiful. I'll see you tomorrow.'

Maria waved them goodbye, like a wise mother who stays behind, shaking her head.

He cycled with her. She lived in Maria's old room, a long way off.

'I can go alone, you know,' she said.

'Of course. I will accompany you up to your front door.'

They cycled next to each other without talking. Agnes was never shy for words, but now she did not know what to say. René was *so* critical!

Before the door he locked his bike to a lamp-post.

'Well, thanks.' she said suggestively.

He came closer. He was a little taller than her, she realised, surprised. She had always thought of him as a little chap. She saw his glance and knew what would happen. Should she allow him or refuse him? And Maria? He grabbed her roughly by the arm and pulled her against him. What a passion there was in this guy! To allow or repel? She thought his attack was exciting….

She felt his lips on hers and tasted the taste… of a man!

'What shall we do about Maria?' she asked René the next morning in bed.

'She's my best friend,' he said with a sigh. 'I'll just tell her.'

'She's also *my* best, dearest friend. She won't understand, René. Or she *will*, but will disapprove. And Maria's disapproval is really dreadful.'

'I know that. But she has no right, none.'

'You're angry because of her constant rejection of you. Is this your revenge?'

He pulled her ear harshly, too harshly.

'Shut up, Agnes,' he said bitterly. 'You're just as beautiful as she is and you were there for the grabbing. I'd have been crazy if I hadn't tried.'

'If you want another time,' Agnes said while she rubbed her red ear, 'you must cut your hair and put on some decent clothes; you are a skunk.'

He jumped out of bed, dressed himself angrily and walked out, slamming the door behind him.

With lead in her shoes Agnes walked to Maria's. She was eating again, but this time she was alone. She evidently did not know yet.

How could you be scared of your little sister?! Agnes kept putting off telling her but finally it had to be said.

'Maria….' she said, hesitating.

Maria looked at her, her blue eyes clear and innocent.

'I slept with René last night…'

Maria seemed untouched and merely asked:

'Are you in love?'

Agnes burst out laughing.

'In love! There'll never be a girl in love with René! He's a repulsive, unsociable skunk.'

Now Maria got angry.

'Then why, Agnes, why in God's name did you sleep with him?!'

'Because it was exciting. That has nothing to do with love, you know.'

'You are sick,' said Maria sternly. 'You are a tart. A real stupid tart. You understand nothing about life! René is a lonely seeker, Agnes. Lonely. You're not going to make him think that there is something between the two of you. Remember that!'

'Who do you think you are, Maria? If he takes the initiative, let him!'

'I know him better than you. I know him through and through. Only a *good* wife can mean something to him.'

'So what're you waiting for, Maria?!'

'I'm looking for love. A total sympathy for someone. That's not possible with René. But I want him to find a good partner.'

'I wasn't planning on becoming his partner. I just slept with him.'

The bell rang.

'There he is,' Maria said and went off to open the door.

He had had his hair cut short and was wearing a new pair of jeans with a light blue shirt. René now looked like a nice, fresh boy. He walked over to Agnes and kissed her on her lips like she was already his.

'Have you already told Maria?'

'Yes,' she said.

He turned to Maria and asked:

'And? Are you angry?'

'Yes. But you mustn't think that I'm jealous. You're a couple of idiots. But do your worst, do that, by all means. Now get out, both of you!'

She opened the door of her room and waited with glittering eyes.

'Out!' she screamed.

René stroked Agnes on her bottom and with the same hand he caressed Maria's cheek in passing. She hit away his hand and stamped her foot.

'Bugger off!'

The door slammed behind them.

'She can get angry!' René said while they got on his bike. 'Come on, I'll take you home.'

René had something. It was his all-pervading negativity. It rejected, but also attracted.... He was not completely harmless, but was quickly hurt and then became violent. Agnes liked to play with such a fire...

In front of the door he locked his bike again.

'You think you already possess me,' she said provocatively. 'Tonight I am not in the mood.'

'Oh yes, you are,' he said. He embraced her and picked her house key from her pocket. He opened the door and made a mocking gesture.

'Go ahead, madam.'

She stood still. She saw that he had got mad. Well, she was not afraid of anything. Never. Not even of farmer Erens. But no one had ever hurt her. René did. He grabbed her by the arm and kicked her across the doorstep.

'I don't stand nonsense,' he said tight-lipped and closed the front door; the key disappeared in the pocket of his new jeans. She was still not afraid, although she fell against the stairs across the doorstep. She got up and walked upstairs.

'Wait until we are upstairs,' she mumbled.

She felt how he came after her threateningly. But once they were in her room, he embraced her and kissed her.

'I love you, Agnes,' he whispered. 'You are mine, now and forever. Mine, do you hear me?!'

She should just let him....

She did not talk to Maria for two weeks. During that time she became completely addicted to René. He was a nerd and a nag, but he was not to be trifled with. She could no longer get rid of him. He did not take no for an answer. She had simply said yes and that had consequences. She was confronted with the consequences every day. He forced himself upon her and when she resisted, he became violent. He did not beat her, but pinched, kicked and pulled her hair. She was never frightened, but thought that his passion was exciting and fought back. She did not think about the future, otherwise she probably would have become desperate. She enjoyed the moment, and the rest would come later. But then, after two weeks, they went home for a weekend, she and Maria. They had already fixed that date earlier.

Maria acted cool and distant when Agnes tried to make contact with her. In the train, when they sat opposite each other, she asked:

'Have you seen René lately?'

'I see him every day, at school. Inescapable.' Maria avoided her glance. 'You can't get rid of René just like that.'

'And what does he say?'

'That you are his girlfriend. And a lot more. He wants to know everything about you.'

'And what do you say?'

'I keep quiet.'

'But he is good at getting his way.'

'Not with me.' She looked at Agnes now, with her stern look. 'Not with me, Agnes.'

'But I do like him,' said Agnes defensively. 'He is very direct; I like that.'

'He's jealous and selfish. And critical. He had nothing at home, not like us. His parents don't live for him, but for all kinds of other things. He's neglected, but not pitiable. Watch out for René. I *know* him.'

'I know a side of him that you don't.'

'Have fun with it.'

'So why are you friends, then?'

'He does have depth. He's a great musician and he thinks very deeply. I've learned a lot by being around him. He did have girlfriends in the meantime, but always only for a short time. He's quickly bored and then he jilts them.'

'Not me.'

'That's what I am afraid of.'

'What do you mean, Maria? Why are you so angry?!'

Maria looked at her emotionally.

'Because there's no love between you! You hate each other, I think that's *sick*!'

'Do you think he hates me?' Agnes asked, scared. She kept silent. Did she hate René? Perhaps; she despised him anyway. She liked him when he became strong and masculine. He became a black knight, not harmless, but forever faithful to his noble woman in the tower. In the tower... forever.... Well, all nonsense. Fairy Tales. She shivered and said:

'I don't hate him, he has something. Let me be, Maria!'

'I *am* letting you be, I can't do otherwise. I love you, Agnes... and I love René a little bit too.'

'So it's okay then?'

'No... it makes me sad.'

'Perhaps you're a little bit in love with him, after all? If so, I'll let him go straightaway, Maria.'

'You don't understand at all. I am worried. You'll have a miserable life. And you can get much better than him.'

'I'm not going to marry him, you know.'

Maria kept silent. She took a book and read for the rest of the trip, apparently very interested in what she was reading.

Ave verum corpus
....
Esto nobis praegustatum
In mortis examine.

The study was heavy going for Maria. She easily pulled through all the exams, but along the way an abyss started to open up between her knowledge and the reality of the human body. Before, when she did not know so much, that abyss was not there, or she had not noticed it. The more she knew about the construction and function of the body, about pathology and the different diseases that can occur, the more insecure she became. Along the way she got the feeling that she could never *dare* to be a doctor, because of the absolute insecurity of her knowledge.

René pulled in Kant, saying:

'The body is 'Ding an sich' (a thing in itself). We'll never be able to see through that. We only have a complex number of deductions in our imagination in relation to the Ding an sich. The other is not reachable, neither the other man in his being, nor the body as it is essentially.'

She felt misunderstood. This was not what she meant at all.

René used her powerlessness to give her another lecture about philosophy. No, she thought that all observations on which knowledge is based indeed have reality value, but she missed the line of connection between her knowledge and reality, while the abyss seemed to get deeper and wider every year. Agnes did not understand her at all. She enjoyed acquiring that knowledge, which extended her self-esteem. She showed it off, like she did with her flexible body and her big brown eyes. She *liked* to be that intelligent beauty, who she imagined herself to be. She completely ignored the college philosophy that René gave out; she did not even listen to it.

Maria passed her examination for her doctoral degree and was completely alone with her insecurity. She seemed to be the only one who suffered from it. She had once made an attempt to talk about it with a dean, but he gave her the feeling that she was deranged and neurotic, a weakling. Finally, she talked about it with her father. He happened to have little *knowledge*, and she doubted if he would be able to understand her.

Like old times they sat in the summer sun on a tree stump in the orchard, and he listened attentively. When she had finished talking, he kept silent for a while, but then said:
'I believe that I can sense what you are going through, child. For I saw you when you were a child – and I see you now. You were a beautiful child, Maria. Full of astonishment and attention for everything around you. Your attention was amazing. You saw and heard everything; you tasted the atmosphere and the happiness and the misery of the people around you. You were always busy and willing to help when we asked you to. A happy, skipping and

still earnest child. I've seen you going to school, how you enjoyed studying. You saw value in that .... I saw how you loosened yourself from nature here, from the growing and blossoming around you. It had to be like that, Maria. Now you're wise, you know far more than me... but you have made a sacrifice for that – you had to make it. Now you live in your knowledge and it's separate from that growing and blossoming of nature. I *see* that, Maria. I don't need thick philosophy books for that. You've become even more noble than you already were, believe me. You've gone beyond the corporeality... but in doing so, you've also lost intimacy. I see great beauty in your soul, child. But with the characteristics of death. A pallid beauty. You're too sensitive not to be aware of that, Maria. Agnes leads a wild life; she gives nothing a moment's thought. She keeps her knowledge close to her body, I see that. She cherishes her knowledge and her body. For her the troubles lie in life itself. Believe me when I say that she'll have a hard job with that René of hers. Your task is not there; it's in finding the way back to nature, while keeping hold of your knowledge.'

Emotion brought tears to Maria's eyes. He understood her so much better than she did herself. He just looked – and listened attentively... and lived in reality.

He put his weathered hand on her knee.

'How is your faith, Maria?'

She shivered.

'Knowledge also expels faith. When I start to *think*, I can't keep my faith upright. Still, there is a firm faith deep down, dad.'

'What is that?'

'That Jesus Christ was truly on earth, that He was the Son of God and that He has risen from the dead. I want to unite both worlds, dad - the world of deep faith and the world of faithless scholarship. It must be possible, mustn't it?'

'Perhaps it is the same abyss, child. The abyss between your knowledge and the physical body and the abyss between your knowledge and your faith.'

'Ave verum corpus,' she said.

'What're you saying, my child?'

'René introduced me to classical music. You'll recognize this song when you hear it. It's often sung in church, it's even almost trite. But it's one of the most touching pieces of music that I know, through the combination of the text and the music. Hail, true body!

Must I now just start with the internships? Jump in at the deep end, in spite of the insecurity? Or must I give up and work in a laboratory?'

'It seems an unnecessary question to me.'

Maria sighed deeply. He knew that she had no less knowledge or skills than anyone; her self-consciousness was only greater, through which she became aware of things that others passed by. She just had to go through with it.

She lacked love. She was not lonely; there were friends, and she had Agnes and René. Her social life was rather too busy than too boring. But there never flamed up in her something of that total love for a boy, for a man. Boys fell in love with her, but she could not answer that love if she did not completely feel it. In her memory she had that one love... there did not seem to be another one possible. Around her, friends became couples, while she remained alone. Well, she loved her family and her friends. But the exclusive love for and of one man was missing. Someone to share her deepest desires with, to have all details of her life in common with.

During the conversation under the apple trees her father asked:

'How about love, Maria? Is there still no man in your life?'

She sighed very deeply, as if she was breathing out her whole soul.

'I believe I am too demanding. I can't respond to the advances of a boy like Agnes can. I loathe it. Agnes says I am squeamish, but I don't believe that it has anything to do with that. I hate the kind of love-hate relationship she has with René. Does she love him? I don't think so. She thinks that he's exciting, so nicely complex and jealous and suspicious as he is. I believe that he's the only one she feels unequal to, and she enjoys that. She makes him weak with her hassling, he becomes weak... and then she strikes! Then she gets beatings and she has the wonderful feeling that she has a *strong* man! I don't understand that at all. I would've had a conversational relationship with René, with a little bit of sex on the side, because I would have to. But nothing in René appealed me. I do care about him a lot, but not like that. Can you understand that? I think that I'm destined to be alone, I expect too much.'

Her father kept silent for a while, in quiet consideration. Then he said:

'There is no romanticism left these days. You don't know how to cultivate love, from the seed to the fruit… You are afraid to exaggerate; to be not normal enough. That leads to excesses as with Agnes, who is, of course, actually in search of security and romance. And with you… you can't find love at all. In love you find the highest, the most beautiful, the best in the other – while you turn away from the weaknesses that everyone has. You young people look at a man in plain reality, you look, listen and so on… and you see all kind of things that you don't like, so it doesn't work anymore. Or you are charmed by the trivial side of a man and you end up in marital fights – whether you are married or not.'

He pointed upwards.

'When you look at these apples, Maria… you won't find one apple that is perfect. We would starve if we had to wait for that. Still, there are beautiful apples and the *whole* tree, with the rotten and ripe apples, is a beauty of creation. On the other hand, love is not something to force. Perhaps this one man still has to come for you…'

They sat quietly next to each other, until her mother called them for dinner.

No romance. Perhaps it was the first time in her life that she had noticed that her father was critical. He never was; he always took life as it came. But apparently, he thought this was really terrible: the disappearance of romance. He did not mean a dinner by candlelight, or a beautiful lace bra. Nor an evening at the cinema in a beautiful dress. Romanticism… what is romanticism?

Back in Amsterdam she looked it up in the encyclopedia and found names like Schelling, Novalis and Goethe, Wagner and Bruckner. Well, her father knew none of them. Still he had a knowledge that went beyond knowing names. What he had meant must have been the same as what was meant by such as Novalis or Schelling. The words 'Weltschmerz' (world-weariness) and 'Sehnsucht' (yearning) aroused intense emotions in her… just the words! She felt touched by a world of feelings that was much bigger than the personal world.

'Novalis is the pioneer of the Romantic.' she read. After a long search she found a copy of *Die Lehrlinge zu Saïs* (The Novices of Sais) by Novalis. It cannot be repeated here what she read… whoever gets bogged down in the sobriety of our Western life, should occupy himself with Novalis' writings. They are a blossom of our European culture, even though at first it might take a little effort to get used to the language and content… because our modern intellect has removed us from the roots of the existence.

Maria did not understand every word she read, for it was a confrontation with a thinking which she too had left behind. Still, she felt what her father had meant by 'romanticism'. It had to be the reinventing of *qualities*. Without noticing it, your thinking gets stuck in quantitative forms and you lose quality. She used to be strongly connected to everything the senses yield of beauty to a child. The

Limburg countryside really was a paradise for that, and the farm that was her home, a private paradise. Everything was very beautiful there, even the weathered tree stump on which they always sat and talked, or the rusting garden chairs between the planters....

She remembered how she had enjoyed the canals of Amsterdam in the beginning, the trees alongside the sunlit facades of the canal houses. Now she saw this beauty only now and then; mostly, her whole existence was aimed at what *had* to be done and a lot had to be done. She felt intensely how materialism obscured *quality*. Not a materialism like capitalism, but a penetrating view of life deep in man that nests inside you unconsciously and removes you to the sobriety of life, to the conviction that *matter* is the only reality in the world. Agnes solved the problem with erotica, but Maria could not do that; she would have felt completely ridiculous.

Inside her, a presentiment awakened from the depths of her soul: she had a long, long way to go. Where that path was heading, she did not know, she had no defined goal in mind. How she had to go along the path, she did not know either. But inside her, she felt that she was at a crossroads.

Perhaps she took life too seriously? Was she not able to play like a child, had everything to be perfect before it could be accepted? Should she not just try something here and there, now and then? In the ugliest man could be hiding a sympathetic being. She was almost twenty four years old; all the boys had girlfriends, all the girls a boyfriend....

With a friend she took a trip abroad for the first time. She wanted to celebrate one way or another that she had made it through her doctoral studies. They were allowed to borrow a car, loaded it full with camping gear and drove to the south on a sunny morning in August.

Annette had just broken up with her boyfriend....
In this holiday 'it' should happen after all. The first day of the trip was nothing special, but after that the landscape started to change. The vegetation took on a particular southern character and along the road there were oleanders and palm trees. Romanticism... here it would be easier to find.

In the hinterland of the French Riviera they found a beautiful spot on a large, busy campsite with a lot of young people. Maria felt how she consisted of 'two souls': one that anticipated this with fear, that hated this... and one that was drawn to it anyway, a slight longing for beauty, luxury and – romance. When they had finally put up the tent, and sat in front of it with a tray of *pommes frites avec salade verte*, she felt a kind of unknown satisfaction. She would forget her restraint for a while and be a little bit more like Agnes....

Annette liked the boys, like Agnes. She had a lot of experience and took Maria in tow. But fantasy was a lot easier than reality. Soon they came into contact with a bunch of

French guys, and soon Annette already had one in mind. A second one came lying close to Maria on the beach. She smelled his sweat and after shave, saw his hairy back and muscles – and was disgusted by it. Did she despise men? No, she also had no need for girls, even less. She shivered. Before her lay three full weeks of sun, sea and beach – and defence. She grabbed a book and said curtly:

'Je veux lire.'

But the boy took her book away from her and put his big hand on her shoulder, and rubbed her back and buttocks. She jumped up and ran into the water....

'How do you do that?' she asked Annette during dinner. How do you make something like that fun? With a guy who's only interested in sex and nothing else?'

'It's exciting, isn't it? I don't get you, Maria. You're such a nice girl. Try to enjoy it for once!'

'That's the problem. It's no pleasure.'

'You must let yourself go, then it'll be fun.'

'I don't want to let myself go.'

She did have fun. She enjoyed everything that could be seen and smelled, the heat and the blue sky, the chirruping crickets, the breathtaking starry sky, the frightening lightning and the clearing afterwards. But she enjoyed it *alone*. She sat with the group, talked a little with them, drank wine and ate French cheese. Sometimes she allowed an arm around her shoulders and on the last night she even gave him a casual kiss. Perhaps if she could have stayed another three weeks....

In a deep melancholic mood she started her first internship in internal medicine She chose a peripheral hospital, where everything was a little less strict than at the university clinic. But here the disadvantage was that there was not a lot of guidance, you had to find your own way. But she soon discovered that she had been scared for no reason. She could easily do it all, no better or worse than the others. There was only that loneliness that could become even deeper! Was it self-conceit? Did she feel better than the rest? Or was it a lack of social ability? René was the only one with whom she could talk a little about what she was going through.

'I was expecting a lot more from life, René! Is this it now? I'm already tired of it now. Getting up every day, going to work, room visits, new hospitalizations, examinations, meetings… everything at a distance from real suffering, on no account too much involvement, being proud of being a doctor, the prospect of a good income. What's the point in that?!'

'And music, and art? Travelling, love? You could've been my girlfriend, Maria – we could've discovered so much together!'

'You're happy with Agnes, aren't you?'

'That's a different kind of happiness. She doesn't care about such things. She has enough when she has herself, her profession and a little bit of René, now and then.'

He sounded bitter.

'Why don't you break up with her then?'

'I'm crazy about her, Maria! And sometimes I hate her

like hell. She makes my blood boil. But I'll stay with her 'till death do us part'.'

René could become very pathetic. She sighed. It was always like this. She wanted to talk about something, but in the end it was never about her.

'Of course I enjoy all kinds of things, René. But it seems to touch me less and less. At work my mood sinks deeper and deeper. What sense does it make?'

'You're not alive, Maria.'

'What you people call 'living' doesn't attract me. All the things that you worry about, about politics, the environment... it doesn't interest me at all. I am searching for an essence in life – and I can't find it.'

'What did you expect, Maria? How should it have been? Maybe you'll find the essence when you become aware of what you're missing.'

She was touched. René was a true friend. She nodded and said softly:

'I shall do that, René. Ask myself what I'm actually missing.'

When he was gone, she sat for a long time, pondering. It was a common dissatisfaction that tormented her. Her father called her a wise woman. She did not see herself like that, but she did have knowledge. She remembered everything well, as well as what she had learned a long time ago. She faithfully read the magazine for medicine every week, she was precise and concentrated. The internist with whom she was interning had already asked her to be his holiday-assistant. But she did not feel like doing that at all.

She could not stand behind it at all, behind that internal medicine – but neither did she know what else she should do. She criticized internal medicine without an alternative. She could start another study - philosophy or law. Her knowledge would increase, but her dissatisfaction as well. No knowledge in the world would bring her peace. It makes you *empty* inside, you are *worn out* as far as the individual human being is concerned. You do fight your egoism, because in knowing, you must forget your daily self-interest for a while. But *with* that forgetting, you also lose the value of existence. She had become *empty*, but on the other hand, also too *full*. Like compensation for the altruism practised in knowing, you were looking for lust, for luxury. Her father did not need that; she did. She longed for a job with decent pay, a nice house somewhere outside and a car of her own. Money to go out for dinner and to travel…. Those were not primary needs, but the consequences of an intellectual existence. Most of all, she longed for a partner, for a man. A friend to share her life with, in all its details. But if she had one, she would still be dissatisfied. He would also not be able to supply the thing she lacked, because it was inside herself. She was not able to quench her thirst for all that is temporary. Everything is temporary after all; you long for the permanent, for something that will never abandon you. A good marriage is an image of that, but there must be an underlying archetype, a truth that she longed for, but did not know how to search for it, or where to find it. It was all too uncertain…. She only knew one thing: if she could understand which crossroads she was standing at, she would choose the surest road, even if it was the longest one.

The candle on her table had almost burned down; she blew it out. She should go to sleep.

She did the psychiatric internship together with René. He wanted to become a psychiatrist. People have affinity with what they need, Maria thought. She loved René very much, but just because of that, she saw his jealousy, his suspicion and sometimes… his meanness. He did know that himself.

'I recognize that paranoid delusion, Maria. With me, the paranoia isn't strong enough to become delusional, but I'm suspicious about everything. If Agnes looks at another man, I check what courses she's doing. If I'd been with you, it wouldn't have been like that, though, from which it becomes clear that my paranoia is based on reality.'

'Maria shook her head.

'No. You would've had that with me too. You don't trust anyone.'

There is no reason to trust anyone. The human being is a rotten creature, with a few exceptions. Agnes is an unreliable woman. If I don't watch out, she goes to bed with other men.'

'Break up with her, then.'

'I'm crazy about her.'

'This is no life! Neither for her.'

René sneered. He threw his head back.

'She's an uncivilized bitch. She lies, cheats and seduces.'

'She's my sister! And *my* parents have raised her. You

know them. You know that they wanted the best for her.'

'That doesn't work with such a girl. She has to have her arse kicked once in a while. That's what has to be done!'

'You're not doing that to her, I hope?!'

He was in a bad mood, René. He laughed at her and exclaimed:

'I do that, and I do more. I'll kill that bitch if she cheats on me!'

Maria shivered. René called out mockingly:

'Your delicate soul shrinks from this, doesn't it? To you everything must be beautiful, noble and right. You don't want the dirt of life. But we're in it up to our necks!'

Maria got angry.

'Keep your stupid mouth shut. You step into that dirt voluntarily. Choke on it then. Let her go out with another man and you kill her with your paranoia! What do I care?'

She got up and banged her chair against the table. All heads turned in the canteen. 'Ooooh!' those faces said. 'Wow!'

She walked outside in anger. She was always seen as the bitch, while those others ranted like animals!

She felt a hand on her shoulder. René. He grinned:

'You're beautiful when you're so angry!'

She turned to him and gave him a smack in his stupid face. Let him kill her too, then!

But he stood there, flabbergasted.

She ran to her bike and pedalled home furiously.

At night Agnes stopped by.

'René told me about today. I thought I'd stop by.' The

81

sound of her voice was timid.

'I didn't know that you and René talked about these kinds of things. I thought that you only have sex and fights,' Maria said coolly. She was more than fed up with it. 'How many times did you cheat on him up to now, Agnes? Tell me, honestly, at least, if you can.'

Agnes sat down, uninvited.

'Come on, Maria.'

'I am asking you a question!'

When she was angry, she always talked to Agnes in dialect; they had grown up like that. It touched Agnes. She bowed her head and said softly:

'A couple of times. I honestly can't only sleep with that nerd.'

'Then why did you even start out with that nerd!'

'He was the one who started it!'

'And you did not know how to say no!'

'I do love him, Maria. More than I loved the other smoothies. He really has something.'

'I'd rather be faithful. Being unfaithful will kill you.'

'You're overreacting. He kicks me now and then, nothing more.'

'Nothing more? Did he ever catch you cheating?'

'No.'

'If that ever happens, he'll kick you to death!'

'Maria, stop it. You know him, don't you?'

'That's exactly why I'm saying this. His depth can become an abyss, into which you'll be thrown because of your stupid, silly behaviour. Either end the relationship or be faithful from now on.'

'I can't live without him.'

'Then stop leading separate lives. For yourself as well as for him. And for me.'

She sat down and buried her head in her hands. Agnes got up and put a soft hand on her arm.

'You're really kind, Maria. Most people aren't like that. You aren't a bitch; we only say that because we're jealous of you. I'm sorry, Maria.'

'The problem is that I never know when you're serious. Or are you playing one of your roles again?'

'Maria!'

She sighed and looked up into her sister's brown eyes. The longing she saw there was at least real. Perhaps it was the same as her own uncertain desire. She nodded.

'Okay. It's okay. But please be careful. And René? Is he angry?'

'Of course not! He was afraid to come here. We are a little afraid of you, you know.'

'Your own conscience isn't speaking loudly enough. You aren't answering my question. Will you be careful?'

Agnes caressed her sister's cheek. The gesture touched Maria, the touch brought tears to her eyes. She missed love so intensely!

They hugged each other intimately, perhaps for the first time completely, real. Maria felt the delicate body of the girl with whom she had so little in common....

'Please be careful with that beautiful, precious possession, your body,' she whispered. 'It's your instrument to express yourself. Please be careful!'

*

After her Bachelor's exam Agnes moved in with René. He could rent half a house at the 'Pijp' through his father. They had their own entrance, a big living-bedroom and their own little kitchen and toilet with shower. Everything was old and dirty, but after some energetic cleaning and painting, it was okay. Soon it became a big mess again, because they were both too lazy to clean or even tidy up. The bed was never made, the table never cleared, clothes were everywhere. In one corner there were Rene's riding boots with his whip in them and his cap on it. In another corner was his cello with the music-stand. The only things Agnes had were clothes and make-up; they were spread around the whole house. It smelled like Rene's shag and Agnes' Sherry. The neighbours could often enjoy hearing the couple's violent rows. But sometimes an almost professional sound could be heard from René playing a Bach cello suite or Agnes' bright laughter, because they also had fun....

The first time that Maria came to visit them, she had looked, perplexed, at the mess that they made. Without saying anything, she had changed the bedding and when she saw that those two were just looking at her doing that, she had handed out assignments. Vacuuming, mopping, scrubbing, washing dishes. In an hour everything was clean. After that, the same thing happened every week....

*

Was Agnes happy with René? She was stuck on him. Or he on her. She made sure that he was well-dressed, cut his hair on time and put him in the shower. So he was pretty nice to look at. He was difficult to handle, easily offended and extremely jealous, but he was not boring; he had profound ideas, worried about the meaning of life, about the violent nature of man, about the existence of God. He read thick books by Freud and Jung, Marx and Steiner. All that knowledge ended up in a big internal soup-tureen, chopped and seasoned. There he made it into his life vision, hot and spicy, but tasty. Furthermore, he liked horses and music. She was meticulously guarded by him; he did not let her out of his sight, except when he went to college and when he had to rehearse or perform with his orchestra. Then she was free – and she used that freedom. She was vain and full of erotic imaginations, which had to be indulged. If she looked at other men when René was around, she got her arse kicked. Mostly only with words, with tirades. She thought he was scary then, but he never hurt her, only a little. During sex he could be very mean, as a reprisal. But she could not resist conquering other men and she did not *want* to resist either. A night with someone else kept life interesting....

In her studies she was ambitious. She was determined to become a surgeon, even though everybody laughed at her. Women did not easily get jobs as surgeons. But she would make it – because she wanted to. She dreamt about a future full of wealth and respect. René and her, both specialists!

At college she asked many questions, so all the professors knew she existed and that she was present. She wanted to be *known* and the knowledge she obtained did not bother her. She was proud of it and tried to surpass everyone. Truth did not exist to her. What you wanted was true. She had an endless supply of lies available – and believed in them herself.

Maria was afraid that René would eventually catch Agnes cheating on him. Agnes wasn't. She outsmarted him and she was not planning on giving in to his possessiveness. Not at all. She was there for all the men, and all the men were there for *her*. No one could resist being seduced by her. No man.

Sometimes she went home for a weekend. René always wanted to come with her, so he went.

At home it was strange…. Her mother, who always cooked, baked, mopped and scrubbed; her father, who was the silent observer, also when he was working in the garden. They were the only ones in whose company she felt ashamed, ashamed of her behaviour. They saw through her, with their simple peasant wisdom. They were tolerant, they let her be. They did not render judgement. Just because of that, their very presence *was* judgement and that was difficult. René seemed like superficiality itself here, with all his knowledge. He became silent and simple here. Quiet and contemplative. That scared her. Perhaps he would see her through her parents' eyes and see through her lying nature. She knew very well that Maria was right. He would use vi-

86

olence. Killing her seemed exaggerated, but a terrible fight would occur – and as a woman she was weak. She might need to go to karate and learn tricks to defend herself. If he ever found out about her cheating, she would then be able to defend herself. In Amsterdam she never had such fears, but they occurred to her in the serenity of the farm in the middle of these fields and under the eyes of her innocent parents.

At night in the big bedstead – they were allowed to sleep together – René said:

'It's like a convent here. Here you don't have to ask yourself if God exists; he exists. I don't understand how such a corrupt creature like you could've been born from such purity.'

She kept silent, offended.

'You are, aren't you, Agnes? You're ambitious, egoistic and a liar. No virtues, right? Have they never seen that?'

'They see it more than anyone, you moron! That's why we are together between this starched linen and not separate. Then we would have to come together secretly; now we don't have to. It was always like this. Here sin is not necessary.

'Then why're you such a sinner, Agnes?'

'What're you talking about? I'm no worse than you.'

'Yes, you are. If I ever have a daughter like you, I'll beat her so often on her naked bottom until her bones know what is allowed and what is not allowed.'

'And I thought that you were so alternative. So modern.'

She snuggled up coyly against him.

'Be nice, René! You hate me!'

He pulled her head back by pulling her hair, and kissed her passionately.

'Hatred is the best basis for sex,' he grinned.

The next morning she stood naked in front of the mirror and observed her body attentively. It showed bruises where he had pinched her. He was still in bed and looked at her beauty with pleasure.

'You're a depraved woman,' he said contentedly. 'Look at how much you like to look at yourself. You're not ashamed of your nudity.'

'There's nothing to be ashamed of. I look superb. Except for these bruises. Proof of your hatred.'

She shook her black hair backwards; it fell richly over her back. She stretched her arms high above her head.

'Go on like that a little,' René said, annoyed, and he got up. 'I'm going to take a bath. It's all too dirty for me.'

He always spoiled the fun. A real man would not have been able to control himself now. He did; he took a bath – which he hated so much.

She sat with her father on the tree stump beneath the apple tree. They had not put a decent garden bench here after all these years. You were broken after sitting here for a while. Nevertheless, she had looked for her father in the garden herself, in a longing for the past....

'A man is always mistaken,' he said thoughtfully. 'I could never have imagined that you would come home with such a man. A rich banker with a Porsche or something, that's what we expected. Not such a critical, deep thinker like René.'

'Don't you like him?'

'I have never not liked anyone, child. All people are worthwhile. I think that you may learn a lot from him. He is developed. I hope that you're good for him too.'

'I'm not a woman like mom,' she said, annoyed. '...a woman who dedicates her life to husband, children and farmstead.'

'You know as well as I do that's not what I mean. I really know what kind of woman you are – that's just why I'm saying this.'

'If you like all people, you must like me too....'

He put his arm around her shoulders.

'But child... you are my daughter.'

'So different from you, from Maria.'

'You have very many qualities. You work hard in your studies, you are healthy and beautiful, watchful and intelligent.'

She sighed. He truly only wanted to see the positive sides. Did he not see her other side?

'And what about my flaws, daddy?' She could see that he was moved by what she had said. He was getting old... his hands were weathered by the open air and the rough work. But his head grew old beautifully. A fan of laughter lines around his eyes, a serious mouth that could also laugh cheerfully.... Now she thought that his eyes had become moist while his arm remained around her shoulders.

'Those are your business, Agnes. We raised you, but now you're a grown woman. You have to raise yourself – if you want to.'

'I never think about that, except when I am here – and

89

with Maria. It's easy for you, you just *are* like that.'

'We also fight, Agnes – but we fight. You can also let yourself go. Talk to mom. She's very worried. She's a little frightened of René.'

He let go of her. She felt like crying and did not know why. She hated women who cried. She thought it was weak. She swallowed her tears and got up. Wiping the dust off her pants, she stood upright.

'Okay dad. I'll go to her.'

She walked towards the farmstead, while her father followed her with his eyes.

Her mother sat at the table peeling potatoes.

'Hey, mom. Can I help you?'

'Come and sit with me for a while. I miss you,' she said.

Her mother had thick working hands and a reddish, countrywoman's face. She had been a real mama, on whose large breasts you could cry when you fell over, or when you had a fight with your sister. She was an excellent storyteller and distracted your sadness by her stories without you noticing. In her stories, which she made up on the spot, magical things always happened; there was magic and there was always a battle between good and evil. That was not possible anymore, but her rich fantasy kept her young, like a little lady from a fairy tale, a good fairy. But they punish you severely when you are lazy or bad… not mom, she remained cheerful and full of trust.

She just put the cards on the table at once and asked:

'Mom, why are you afraid of René? Dad says you are.'

She put the peeler and the potato down and leaned backwards. She took a deep breath and shook her head.

'The way he looks at you. It makes me feel uncomfortable. I know such people, they are profound but quickly hurt and then they become aggressive. I don't think that's the man for you. You must have someone who understands you. Not someone who suffers from who you are. That's not right for either of you.'

'Don't you believe in fate, mom? In my dreams I also imagined something else, a handsome prince charming on a white horse, who comes to save me. Real life gives you a man who you'll have to share your life with, whether you want to or not. Of course I want to, but he isn't something like my great love.'

'You should've waited for that then.'

'I couldn't. Look at Maria, she keeps on waiting....for something that never comes.'

'Hurry never leads to anything good.'

'It's no hurry. It's fate, destiny perhaps. I can't do it differently.'

Her mother took the peeler and started peeling again.

'It's your life,' she said, satisfied with that.

You couldn't possibly be angry with mom and dad. Everything consisted of love here, you could only flourish here....
Her mother said:

'If you think that we're naïve, Agnes – then you're completely wrong. We *knew* what you were doing on those Friday nights. We let you go your own way on purpose, because we thought that was the best thing to do. You must understand that.'

Agnes was startled by the sharp tone. Did she think her parents were naïve? She shrugged.

91

'I'm not an easy person, I know that.'

Her mother went on peeling in silence. Despite her mother's disapproving attitude, Agnes stayed beside her. She looked around and saw the old shiny stove, the freshly washed traps alongside the shelves, the sanded pans and spoons. It was a kind of a convent that she had grown up in; it was nothing like her, this peace. She had to acknowledge to herself that she liked the battlefield more, the frontlines, the trenches, and the danger of death....

On the train back to Amsterdam they sat opposite each other in silence. After an hour of silence, Agnes asked:

'Why are you just sitting there? You could say something!'

'You aren't saying anything either. What is there to say? Staying there is like the last line in a sentimental comic story: 'Love can only live, life can only be good, where, , everyone does everything for the other, silent and unconstrained.'

'Pah. You are mocking it.'

'It's unbelievable, isn't it? It can't be true. Deep in the unconsciousness of those people there must also be crap, right? Didn't they live through the war? Do they live in imaginations?'

However, she had had such thoughts herself many times; now she got angry because he had them. She said:

'They are honest; they always *have* been. You and me – we're of a different kind; we don't know their world. We do from the outside, but not from the inside.'

'They have no clue about *life*, Agnes! They don't *know* anything. They live with apples and cherries, with God and commandments. They don't know the big world. Otherwise they would've taught you something. You didn't learn anything there, did you?'

'What do you know about it, René? Do you know what I'd be like if I'd had different parents? Yours for example, who neglected you because they were so busy getting to know the big wide world? You haven't a *clue* how good I had it at home!'

René gave her an angry look and was silent again.

At home she unpacked her bag and hung everything neatly in the closet. She was fed up with his endless negativity, his digging in the dunghill of existence.

'What a sweet housewife!' he mocked. He stood behind her and wrapped his arms around her middle, so she could not move.

'I'm sick of you!' she said. 'Really sick! You paralyze everything in a human being with your constant criticism.'

He pinched her belly viciously. She tried to release herself, but he was too strong.

'Stop it, René, stop it! I'm going to go and look for an apartment. I don't want to be with you anymore!'

With his knee he gave her an enormous push, and she fell against the sink.

'If you ever dare leave me, I'll kill you!' he screamed. 'I'm leaving now. Clean the place up if you wish. But if you're not here when I return, I'll find you wherever you are!'

He slammed the door behind him and dashed down the stairs. He was going to Maria, sure he was. She walked into the bedroom and fell on the bed. If only she could just leave now? She shouldn't let herself be forced? He had a big mouth and a tiny heart. Kill her?… Nonsense! But she did love that tiny heart. He repelled her, but also attracted her irresistibly. Perhaps it was the permanent threat of a beating that made her stay. Not the fear of it, but the longing for it. He never did it, but there was always the threat of it in the air. Perhaps she loved that. No, she also loved *him*, his incomprehensible being. The fact that he apparently cared for her, whatever that may be. The sex they had, that was always good…. He loved her passion, but also wanted to restrain it; that made for the tension between them. She longed for him *now*, she was actually too proud to keep waiting here. She could hardly be here when he returned, as if she had obeyed him. But if he came home and she was not there….? She did not know how serious he had been. She could also go to Maria's and pick him up there. She was lonely, so lonely…. René was still the only one with whom she really had something, a community…. She could never leave him; she did not want that at all. Perhaps she was waiting for the moment when he would be really nice to her. He never was – and she actually liked it. Imagine having a *kind* man next to you! She would go crazy! She turned on her belly and hugged her pillow. She would wait for him nicely, let's see what he will do…

She had to wait for a long time, too long. Se fell asleep on the bed and woke up when she heard him throwing up in the toilet. He had drunk too much, but was not even really drunk. He put the light on and looked around.

'You haven't made much progress in tidying up. What a mess!'

94

She got up and said angrily:

'As if you give a damn! Where've you been?'

He breathed his drunken fumes in her face.

'At the pub. I thought: I'll come home late. Then she'll have enough time to come home again.'

She got off the bed.

'I didn't leave at all. I've been waiting for you all the time. You don't get it.'

She hid her head in the pillow. As harsh as he could he hit her on her backside. The bed bounced.

'Why did you do that?' she complained and stayed on the bed as if asking for more. He turned away and mumbled:

'Because I hate you. I *hate* you, you stupid bitch!'

She did not know whether to cry or flatter – or walk away. Tactics. You had to have tactics. She was too tired for tactics.

'What's wrong?' she complained.

'What's wrong!' he imitated her. 'You were fed up with me, remember?'

'Ah, you're offended....'

He took off his clothes and pulled a blanket off the bed from beneath her.

'I'll go and sleep on the couch. You disgust me,' he said coldly.

'As if that isn't an insult!' she said. She jumped up and started a small strip-tease. But he put off the light and crawled on the couch beneath his blanket.

Longingly, she stayed behind… a lonely soul, not knowing how to handle it all.

,Give me matter
And I shall build you a world out of it.'

Immanuel Kant (1724-1804)

After Maria graduated she went back home, to Limburg's hill country. She had still not found her way in her profession; her enthusiasm for it was completely paralysed. In Limburg she could get a job as an infant centre doctor. With that she would earn her living, be able to buy a nice little house and that would be her life then. She would have her beloved nature around her and her parents nearby. She was also happy to be rid of Agnes and René, who demanded so much of her attention that she had become really tired of it. They were always fighting, made a mess of everything in every way and looked to her as the angel of peace and as the cleaning lady.... Now there was only the phone and a meeting once every few weeks. Maria had the feeling that she could finally start to live for herself.

She was confronted more and more with the transience of life on earth. Everything you experienced eventually became a memory, and what was more brief and blunt than remembrance? Finally, death would also end that. Because all you have in your memory comes from observing with the senses. Memory images are sensory images. What if the body falls into decay with its senses? What remains then…

a vague emotional life? But feelings for what then, if there are no senses left to observe? You may be God-fearing and believe that the soul lives on after death... but what content has that soul if there are no senses anymore? Without any senses to serve the mind.... nothing remains then, does it? She had learned to think such thoughts from René. But she saw nothing in his solutions. She thought he was rash in his conclusions; he did not think his opinions through and because of that, he did not see the constant contradiction in it. He could become enthusiastic for the most diverse ways of thinking; that was one of his charming characteristics. But he forgot about the previous notion with the same convenience as he accepted the next one. He never tried to find uniformity in that abundance. She thought that such a way of thinking was an example of the transience of notions.... They are there as long as you keep busy with them; they fade as certainly as the transitory sensory impressions. Transience.... She saw transience in everything.

She loved her parents very much, but she had to see them grow older... well, they were not really old, not yet sixty... but the transience was nevertheless visible. Mother scrubbed less fanatically, bought a pie at the bakery now and then instead of making it herself.... Her father had a ranch hand for the heavy work; he sat more and longer musing beneath the apple tree, or in the winter by the stove in the kitchen. She suspected her father had a rich inner life; he was not dozing off or snoozing. He was contemplating. But his contemplations also seemed to have a transitory character.... they were based on the gospel or on learned prayer. Neither could remain if the instrument, the body, ever fell away?

She was therefore often in a melancholic mood, as if her mind was made of apple blossom that was starting to wither.... She lived with her parents again temporarily, because she still had to look for a suitable house. She wanted to live somewhere in the countryside in a little detached house with a garden and a nice view....

It was strange to come back to the silent Limburg countryside after all these years in Amsterdam. She had longed for it, but now she already felt that she would feel nostalgia for the city. You would not run into people like René here. It was quiet, but also boring.... Here, one lived from nature, silence, all very pleasant. There, life was full of spirit, busy, fascinating. Apparently, they could not go together.

She drove through all of southern Limburg with a broker, looking for a nice house. The prices were favourable; she earned a good salary and should be able to find something nice. The broker was a nice young Limburg man, fresh and well-dressed. With astonishment, she noticed that she was attracted to him. He smiled a lot, spoke in dialect with her and drove really sharply along the winding roads. On his ring finger he had a smooth golden ring....

At night in bed she asked herself, what had made her feel attracted to such a young man.... It was the fresh happiness, the uncomplicated view of life, the daring to just *be*. No socialism, Freudianism, materialism or whatever ism. Enjoying youth and beauty, the good fruits of life... the optimism of simplicity. No doubt she would get as bored by that as by the inevitable beauty of the landscape in spring. Summer, autumn and winter have to follow spring over and over again... nothing can ever remain the same.

She found a house in a village street, small and old-fashioned, but with a very deep garden. The garden made her decide to buy the house: something could be made of it. The first thing she did was plant an apple tree in the back of the garden. From a tree stump from her father's garden she made a bench to sit on underneath the tree. From that corner in her garden the rest of the garden would grow.... Her father's ranch hand helped her hang the wallpaper and paint the rooms....

In November she moved into the house, René and Agnes and her parents were there to help her. In the evening they had dinner together round the big table in the kitchen.

'And now, a man.' René said, contemplating, when they were having coffee after dinner. 'I don't understand that the most beautiful woman in the world is still single.'

'You hurt everyone with such a comment,' Maria said angrily.

He tapped Agnes's leg.

'She knows how it is. She's certainly not jealous of her sister.'

'Still you don't have to say something like that,' Maria said while she looked at her sister inquisitively. Agnes shrugged and said:

'We know who's saying it, Maria. You're waiting for your knight in shining armour; perhaps you're right.'

'Look, I can never let a man dominate me; that's the first problem. There should be absolute equality. I do meet emancipated woman, but I must still meet a man who is fully willing to accept equality. Except for daddy, you're from a different world. Ordinary men are unintentional rulers. You too, René. You above all.'

'Lay off,' grumbled René. 'I'm a soft egg, you know that, Maria, don't you?'

'Self-knowledge is a rare talent,' said Maria. 'As an upcoming psychiatrist you should develop that talent.'

'She never minces words,' René complained, turning to her parents. 'She just says it right in your face.'

Her mother giggled.

'Come on, boy, have another drink. You talk too much.'

All the talk was trivial, but still Maria felt a whole world between them. What was it? Why did she always stay behind in longing, because that world never truly appeared; it floated around nothing and nowhere. If she had been a man a couple of centuries ago, she would have challenged René for a duel....at five o'clock in the morning, in a remote place. Why? Because he was just the way he was. A prevalent pain in the arse. He treated her sister badly – who indeed asked for it, but still. He was still whining about the fact that she, Maria, had rejected him, and that he had to be satisfied with her twin sister. That was an impossible task for Agnes too....

Maria got up. 'Come,' she said decisively. 'I have to experience how it is to be living alone in a house in a village.'

Alone. Finally, she was alone. She had lived alone for years, in a room in the city. That was something different; she had a goal then. Now she had arrived here. Was this the goal?

The bell rang.

Alone in a house in a street in a village.... Who could that be? René, who had left something behind? Should she even open the door? Well, it was an innocent village, where she lived.

She went to the front door and opened it. A man stood in the dark evening; he was in a panic.

'I'm very sorry!' he gasped. 'I live across the street and I heard that you're a doctor. My parents are visiting me and my mother's become unwell. We've called the local doctor, but he's not answering the phone. Would you please come with me?'

A stethoscope and a blood pressure meter. A case with ampoules and a couple of hypos and injection needles. She still had it all from her GP training. Quickly, she put everything in a plastic bag and followed the man to his house. Now she should not think about her lack of experience, about what could go wrong. Just calmly do your job, like you learned to do it. A young inexperienced doctor is better than no doctor at all....

She saw the rich decoration of the house across the street, even though she was nervous and concentrated on what had to be done. A marble hall, expensive tapestries, thick rugs in the ensuite rooms. Antique furniture ... a couch with an old lady on it and next to her a gentleman in a panic, her husband.

'Oh, doctor, I am so happy that you have come here immediately! My wife is dying under my hands!'

'Please call an ambulance,' she told the son calmly. She knelt down by the lady. She was alive. Her pulse and blood pressure were good, but she groaned with a chest pain. She gave the woman two injections and prayed to God that the ambulance would come soon.

'I think the lady's having a heart attack,' she said. 'But right now there's no direct danger. She must be hospitalized immediately.' She called the heart specialist, boldly introduced herself as a colleague and informed him of the arrival of the old lady. Half an hour later, she was back in her new home, alone again. She sat at the table, took her head in her hands and burst into tears.

The next evening she was sitting alone at the kitchen table, eating some Chinese food. She had worked all day and on the way home she got a Nasi Goreng. She still felt deeply unhappy, a lonely lost traveller in a land with different habits. The bell rang. Feeling bewildered, she went to the front door. The same man was standing in the dark.

'Good evening, doctor. I wanted to come and thank you for your help and ask you for the bill. My mother is in coronary care and she's doing well.

'Come on in for a moment.' she said, relaxed.

She went ahead of him into the kitchen. She wanted to

finish her dinner and forgot that it is strange to welcome a guest into the kitchen.

'It smells good.' he said, smiling.

'Do you want some too? There's enough.'

She took a plate and utensils and a glass.

'A beer?'

What was she doing?! She was in a dream! The man was still smiling and sat down at the table.

'Excuse me, your coat,' she said, took his coat and took it to the hat stand.

Suddenly, she was sitting with a stranger at her even stranger table.

'It's nice here,' the man said politely.

She thought about the expensive Persian carpets and the mood lighting across the street. Did she have no embarrassment anymore? She was out of her mind! But she looked at the man, who was sitting there opposite her. She had looked at him, but not seen him. He wore an expensive grey suit, because of which she had mistaken his age. He was not much older than she was.... She looked at his hands. No rings. It had come this far for her! Gradually, she was looking for a man. 'Now, a man.' René had mocked. Here he was. Already....

'Let's eat,' she said. 'The food's getting cold.'

She lifted her glass and toasted with him. He smiled again.

'I wanted to thank you, doctor. I think it's fantastic that you came immediately. That made such a difference!'

'Without me it would've been fine too,' she resisted.

'You were very calm. It was the calmness of someone who

knows her profession. That's very important when you are in a panic.'

She was quiet and ate. She was shy in his presence and felt free at the same time. It was nice of him that he came by. She did not dare to look at him. There was something about him. A polite air of superiority or something. His dark hair was cut short and he looked well-groomed. A real Dutchman, not a man from Limburg.... A little reserved, affected, abstract. Nothing for her, was her conclusion.

He emptied his plate impeccably and used his napkin before drinking his beer. A civil young man. A boy? A man?

'You're not a general practitioner? he asked politely.

'No. A paediatric doctor. Perhaps I'd like to become a school doctor.

'Too bad. You really worked like a GP, doctor.'

'Please call me Maria, instead of 'doctor'. I don't feel like a doctor at all.'

He smiled. She felt a little frail from his smiles.

'I'm happy that your mother's doing well.' she said.

Again that giant world arose that floats around nothing and nowhere.... Life is so much more than those couple of commonplaces. He had beautiful hands, slender, long fingers.

'What's your profession?' she thought about the marble and the Persians.

'I'm a lawyer. I own a firm at Maastricht.'

'You *own* a firm?'

'I started out a couple of years ago, self-employed. Now it's quite an office.'

'You're not from here.'

'From The Hague.'

'What does somebody from The Hague do in Maastricht?'

Again that smile.

'Hills and valleys. The soft 'g' in the accent.'

She got the tickles from his smile. Was he flirting with her? If that was the case, she did not dislike it. Was this finally romance?

'You must send a bill,' he said.

'Yes, yes. Have you already lived here for a long time?'

'If I may say 'Maria' - let's be on a first-name basis - I've lived here for three years now. It's good here. Quiet... even though everyone interferes in your life. Tomorrow the whole village will know that I had dinner here.'

She cleared the table.

'Do you want a cup of coffee?' she asked him quickly, when she saw that he wanted to get up.

He stayed put and nodded.

She was now three Marias. One who moved very calmly and made coffee, even though she was watched closely, even though she felt his eyes on her back. One who was beside herself from a kind of strange excitement, of which nothing was tangible from the outside – and one who looked at all this astonished and had her thoughts about it. 'This lady is starting to fall in love!' the third, observing Maria thought. The second Maria suddenly felt that she had a woman's body, with all sorts of curves that men like. The first Maria did not express anything of this, poured coffee unaffected and with quick hand, put the cup on the table in front of the smiling man. The smiling boy.

He certainly stayed because he wanted to be polite. To thank her for her help.

He had clear blue eyes beneath thick dark eyebrows. In spite of his perpetual smile there was a wrinkle of sorrow above his masculine nose. The second Maria shivered, the first was impenetrable. Did he have a girlfriend?

'Do You live in that big house all by yourself?' she asked, rather formally.

'You were going to say 'you'! Yes. I've met no woman who meets my requirements. Up to now, at least.'

Are you so special yourself then? she thought, annoyed. But there was also no man who could meet her requirements, right?

'Attractive, intelligent, tender, assertive, sweet....' he enumerated, laughing.

He was laughing!

'Artistic and faithful until death.'

He looked at her, smiling again, very long. She did not want to retreat, but at last looked away.

'I hate domineering men,' she said meaningfully.

'Without prevalence, there is no man – without... compliance, there is no woman,' he said. 'That's just the way it is.' He got up. 'I hate to leave.'

'Then why are you leaving?'

The invisible world between and around nothing would not prevail this time. She would become visible, audible. She got up as well.

'Because that's how it should be,' he said, smiling. 'I came to thank you and ask for the bill, doctor. I've stayed too long already.'

She moved in front of him. One should be bold. The three Marias joined in one strong woman who said:

'Stay a little. I will pour you a cognac, in the living room.'

His smile became more human, more real. She stared at the ground. Without compliance, no woman....

'Okay,' he said and followed her to the living room.

For a moment, a couple of seconds, reality had become master over the illusion. It was a blessing of what one calls love. After that, illusion struck again. They chattered back and forth about all kind of things, except about what it was really about.

When he finally made to leave, Maria forced reality to triumph once more.

He pulled on his winter coat. She wanted to hold him, but now he was really leaving. She said:

'What'll happen now?'

He stood still, astonished. She stood a little astride, upright, ready to fight. He grinned. I do not like domineering men, she thought desperately. But she gave in and smiled.

He leaned over and touched her head with his lips for a moment.

'This is what'll happen,' he said.

He knew how to handle it. He gave her so little that she had to long for more.

'Are you free tomorrow?' he asked, distant again.

She nodded.

'Then I'll take you out for dinner. I can't cook, and I owe you a dinner. I'll ring your bell at 6.30, okay?'

She nodded again, speechless.

He turned around and left.

The first Maria subjected herself to the second. The third watched quietly. She sat down at the kitchen table, took her head in her hands and cried until she was completely empty.

Perhaps for the first time in her life she did her job routinely, while her thoughts escaped her again and again. Does one search for something everlasting in all the transience, in the faithful love for one person? The bodies of two lovers also perish sooner or later – but love? Is it something eternal? Where does it go then? What she felt now, which distracted her feelings and thoughts, was that love? Love of what? Of the appearance of a stranger? Of his smile? His restraint? Of what?

In her lunch break she bought a new dress and shoes. She never went out to dinner, certainly not with a man…. At home she put on a little make-up, she combed her long hair loosely over her shoulders and waited for the doorbell to ring.

Exactly at 6.30 he was standing there in a dark evening for the third time.

'Are you ready?' he asked.

She closed the door behind her.

He was wearing a black turtleneck beneath a grey suitjacket and over it, a leather jacket with a soft lining.

He opened the door of a sports car and helped her to get in. Leather chairs, a walnut dashboard with a couple of meters, a leather steering-wheel. He sat behind the steering-wheel and started the engine. She smelled his aftershave. Tonight he was the great womanizer. He thought he already had the chicken in the pan! Well, that would disappoint him! This little chicken was alive and kicking and would not let herself be caught!

He grazed away.

'Nice car,' she said.

He looked aside. Was she joking?

'A boy's dream. As a kid I played with cars for days. My first word was 'Vroom, vroom!' They are all in a cupboard in my house now. The most beautiful thing is such a car for real of course. But it's not important. For a lack of something better I keep busy with such things.'

'What would be better than this?'

'A beautiful woman.'

'That doesn't seem such a problem.'

'Pretty, intelligent etc. She doesn't exist. At least....'

He drove to an expensive restaurant in Maastricht. She knew it of course, but had never been there before. He parked the car around the corner, where it was forbidden to park.

'You aren't allowed to park here.'

'I always park here. Come on, madam, no worries!'

Was this romance? Certainly not the romanticism of Novalis. A man behind a grand piano played a melody by Rubinstein. Too good to be plain, too bad to be called *music*. The waiters played their show of dedication.... Damask, silver, crystal, flowers and pleasant music. Romance?

She looked very different with her hair hanging loose,

make-up and new clothes, but he did too. Handsome and smooth, used to having lunch and dining in expensive places, quite a talker. No different from the boys that she used to reject. This was cultivating the transience, not conquering it. 'You're too stern, Maria.' René used to say. Was this man better than René? Fresher, brighter, not unworldly, but beside that....

'You're not really having fun,' he noticed disappointedly after an hour. She sighed.

'I can't stand this... thing. I like it and so on, but I already have such problems with everything temporary. Where is the eternal? I don't see it. Here I don't see it at all.'

He put his beautiful professor's hand on hers. She let him.

'I'm a legal expert. That doesn't look good either... but I've also studied a little mathematics in order to train my thinking. Plato thought already at that time that it was a condition for true philosophy.... Of course you only observe temporary things with your senses. But think about Pythagoras' theorem. That has permanent validity; it doesn't change through time. If everything transient is thought away, there are still the basic rules of mathematics.'

She liked what he said. A lot more attractive than the constantly changing principles of René.

'And your law books? That say one is not allowed to drive faster than a hundred kilometres per hour? That's invented nonsense, isn't it? As transient as anything?'

'I think so too. But the basic principle 'Thou shall not kill.'... is in total agreement. That is a permanent principle.'

'The law brings sin… Paul says.'

'Perhaps…. You're an earnest doctor, Maria.'

His hand was still on hers. His blue eyes rested on her without wandering. On her stature, her glance. He truly had something…. Or was it the red wine that warmed her so that she started to enjoy the piano music?

'Perhaps 'stern' is a better word. You may indeed also enjoy life.'

'I do. Beneath the apple tree in conversation with my father. During concerts with René.'

'Who is René?'

'My twin sister's boyfriend. I've known him for a very long time. I also enjoy my work …'

He caressed her hand and asked:

'Have you had a lot of relationships, disappointments?'

'Not one. I'm looking for a man who is handsome, intelligent, sweet and strong. How was it again?' she smiled now. 'And what about you?'

'Yes. I've tried various things. Those beautiful girls, who like to sit in a sports car.'

Time went by too quickly. At a certain moment all the courses were finished, up to the coffee with liqueur. She thought it was a pity….

Outside she shivered from the cold. Back home now….

He put his arm around her shoulder and took her to his car. Now what?

She got in, he got in. She wanted to fasten her seat belt.

'Leave it for a minute,' he said. He took her head in his hands and kissed her carefully. That's the way it goes…. She pushed him away.

'I'm not sure… if I want this.' she said.

'I do,' he grinned and tried again. 'Give in, Maria. You don't have to do anything, we'll take it slowly. Come on'.

She felt tears coming to her eyes. She was looking for everlasting love and was not sure if he could give it to her. She longed for him, but was he who she thought he was?

He jumped from the car and helped her get out again.

'Come on, sweet doctor! We'll go for a walk. Just like that, anywhere. You in my arms, until you can trust me….'

They walked a bit along the Maas, in the icy November cold. He held her tightly and she indeed felt something familiar. Finally, he took her home, to her doorstep.

'How will it go on now?' she asked again.

'I'll call you or I'll stop by.' he said.

Startled, she said:

'Oh no. That's not the way it'll go. I'm not going to sit and wait for a call. We'll make a date now or we will not, not at all.'

They stood in front of her door, the whole street could see them. He grinned and tapped her cheek. She blushed, but it was dark. He said:

'You're not only a stern doctor, but also a very direct one. Come here!'

'You come here!' she said stubbornly.

He took a step towards her and whispered in her ear:

'Tomorrow, at 6.30. And the day after tomorrow. And Thursday, and Friday and so on… until we are eighty, ninety, hundred. Okay?'

'Okay,' she said.

She went inside, put up her coat and did not go to the

kitchen. Straight upstairs, to bed she went. She now had a boyfriend....

He welcomed her into his home. He was wearing a white Norwegian sweater and jeans.

'You show yourself in metamorphoses, first as a lawyer, then as a playboy, like Elvis, and now... as... just a sporty guy.' She looked around. 'You should actually have three houses too. This is the lawyer's house. Then one for the playboy, a brothel or something – and finally a cottage with sheep and apple trees.'

'The third is your house across the street. The brothel is my bedroom, I'll spare you that for now. And this here, yes, this is the house of the lawyer, who travels about, bored, and collects antiques. All worthless, Maria... now that you're here. Give me your kitchen table....'

'What's your garden like? May I see it?'

'It's dark. Come.'

He turned on the garden light. She saw a romantic landscaped garden, with a lot of winter green and a white garden house at the back. No apple tree.

'Assembled by an artist,' he said and put off the light again. He was ashamed of the luxury. Maria had such a radiation that all wealth paled in her presence. But she said comfortingly:

'It's all very beautiful and tasteful. What'll we do now? Go out to dinner at 6.30 for the next sixty or seventy years?'

He shrugged and said:

'Can you cook? I can't.'

'Yes, of course. Do you have anything in your refrigerator?'

'No. But we'll do that tomorrow. Today I'll take you out again. We'll go to Aken and have Sauerkraut.'

She got to know the charm of transience, while at the same time the notion of something lasting grew inside her. Jean saw something in her of which she had never been conscious, but which she recognized now as essentially *herself*. He worshipped that 'something' in her and expressed his regard in attention and romance. She did not know what happened to her. Physically, he took the initiative with a vigor. He asked her out, took her to the opera in Brussels or to an exposition in Liege ... he took her in his arms and kissed her... no doubt that he would decide when she would sleep with him – or was allowed to, she did not really know what she thought about that. But in their contact, in their conversation, he considered her to be an example. He admired her pure judgement, her lack of sympathy and antipathy in her consideration of people and things, her intense questions in life, which she cherished without extorting answers. He was thirty two years old, six years older than her. He had read a lot, asked himself questions about life and death, good and evil, the eternal and the temporal. But in conversation with her, who had little *knowledge* about the possible answers, he felt the worthlessness of all his knowledge. He read Kant, Hegel, Nietzsche and Steiner. He had collected insights, but he admired her for the innocence of her pure questions. She was not looking for answers, she first wanted to become aware of what her questions actually were. She did not think *about* these questions, she *lived* them. If he was worth being loved by her, it was because he acknowledged the high quality of her being, he recognized it. She did not hate the world, but she suffered from its increasingly technical character. She loved people, but longed for real communion. He thought it was a pity that she wasted her great humanity on some inspection work at an infant centre. She had to be a real practising doctor and put her love and compassion at the service of suffering people!

'You really should be a general practitioner, Maria. You'd be a blessing for your profession.'

'I can't, Jean. I'd want to have a lot more real knowledge. I have technical knowledge... but I know nothing about life and death. What is the human being!? What is sickness, what is healing? I know a lot, but I lack real understanding. You've studied your law books, and how laws are the way they are. A car is also how it is, there is no riddle to it. But a human being...? I'm too conscientious to just treat patients and conditions at random. I want to know what I'm doing, what I'm busy with. No-one's been able to teach me that, not even the most learned professor. You talk about mathematics. If I think away the physical human being, am I left with a mathematical scheme? You don't believe that yourself, do you!?'

'Behind those law books there's also the model of good and evil.'

'One has a lot more leverage on that with a pure conscience. An education of the ability to make judgments is enough, then. Not in my profession; there's an abyss between my technical knowledge – that's a part of reality, I also believe that – and the riddles of sickness and healing, death and life, of the living body.'

'You should read Steiner sometime. He has the answers to your questions. I stopped reading him because I thought I was too young and inexperienced for them. Some time in the future, I'll read them again.'

'Ah… Steiner. No. I've seen how people live with that. I saw a cabinet filled with books, but a house which was one big mess. They left their only child to fend for himself, because they were so 'spiritual'. I've never seen more selfishness and ugliness than in that house. But I do understand that that doesn't necessarily say anything about poor Steiner. People simply like to ruin the highest things in life. Still, there's a barren atmosphere, an atmosphere of dereliction around the name Steiner.'

'With him you find the answer to the question of the permanent in the transient. You should forget everything you feel around his name and judge his work purely for what it is. If anyone is able to do that, it's you Maria.'

She smiled.

'First, let me get to know some exuberant life with you, before I may have to give it up. With you now, I'm only just alive. Everything before that was just preparation, emptiness.'

When spring arrived, and the apple tree unfolded its first blossom, she asked Jean to sit with her on the bench.

'If we live in your house, later… you have to plant an apple tree for me, so we can sit there and contemplate the riddles of existence,' she said, melancholically.

'We can also live here, my dearest Maria. Then I'll be your simple boy in a cottage with a couple of sheep and an apple tree. You are my wealth, my everything…. The best dinner I've ever had was that Chinese meal at your kitchen table, on an evening in November. Dinners with candle light, brilliant rings, Persian carpets and an Alfa Romeo… that's all just decor, a method of expression to embody my ecstatic happiness, to show it to you. But an apple tree in Limburg, with a bench for contemplation… to be together with you, something more beautiful than that doesn't exist.

*

Agnes seized a training spot on the surgery ward. She had been a holiday assistant first and had done her best to the extent that she could start the training immediately after her doctor's exam. She had to work hard, put in long days and nights, overcome her resistance, endure critics… but she felt that she was alive, that she was worth something. You had to get used to something that seemed like the discipline of a battlefront. She had to leave her disorder at home and she had to put up with what was necessary from her male colleagues. At home there was always a complaining René waiting for her, with his discontent because she was away so much. Agnes simply lived for herself one hundred percent. René was allowed to be present, but it was all about her, not about him. He had become a shrink; that was easy. She would become a real specialist!

Where she could, she used her exuberant beauty to get them on her side. If she had to, she used her body with ease. René was too stupid ever to find out; she had outwitted him in everything. Still, she would not want another man than René. He was a whiner and sometimes very mean, but they were used to each other and matched each other. In bed he was aggressive, and she liked that. Other men soon bored her...

There was one man to whom she was really attracted - Jean, Maria's husband. He had something that attracted every woman. He was good-looking, strong and successful and on the other hand, he was a knight to his wife. But he was the only one on whom Agnes did not use her tricks. She might be bad and corrupt, but she really loved Maria. She would never hurt her.

When she had worked on the ward for a couple of months, one of the assistants in internal medicine came for a consultation during a nightshift. A large lady had had an operation on her gall bladder, but now her diabetes had become a problem. As a surgeon, she did not know a lot about that, so the consultant on duty had to be called to deal with it. She knew him; he cut a striking figure. Tall, blond, and handsome, but the most distant man she had ever met. He was totally untouched by her beauty. He was only occupied with the lady in the bed, even though *she, Agnes,* was standing there. He was in excellent control of his professional work, but there seemed to be nothing human about him.... Technique, skill, ability and dedication

– but no passion or other personal emotion. One wanted to conquer such a man, make him weak, force an explosion of that controlled passion. She resolved that she would get him into her bed, sooner or later. After all, what she decided on always happened....

During the lunch break he was eating at one of the long tables while conversing with a colleague. She sat down with them and got a friendly nod from them. He asked her:

'How is the lady with diabetes?'

'Until now no problems. You internal medical specialists are always reasoning and calculating. Do you like that?'

He smiled, which gave his seriousness something sunny. His greyish eyes became blue.

'As a human being one is searching for something lasting in what is transient, isn't one? Something that you can fall back on, which is the same in every human being?'

He was of course referring to the chemical and physical laws. But she said:

'The most crushing thing which is the same for all humans is that they all die in the end.'

He became serious again.

'So will you,' he said.

Bam! It felt like he had given her a box on her ears. She looked at him defiantly and said:

'That's another thing that's the same with all people - not wanting to think about one's own transience.'

'People are different in that, Agnes.' Her name felt like a caress when he pronounced it. 'One can also become preoccupied with the riddle of life and death.'

'That's true,' she said compliantly. 'My sister does that; she puzzles her head off.'

'Your boyfriend René also asks himself these questions.'

'How do you know René?' she asked flabbergasted.

'He was an intern here, wasn't he? I was here as an assistant. People said that he had such a beautiful girlfriend. I see now that they were right.'

This was the way it always started… and still she did not feel admiration coming from him. He only ascertained facts, without feeling anything about them. She ate her tasteless food in silence.

He stayed and watched. When she was finished, he asked:

'Do you still have time for a walk?'

She nodded. Together they walked out of the hospital. She felt his cool nearness. What to do with such a guy? She asked:

'Do you have a wife? A girlfriend?'

'No. I think I'm too demanding. And I work hard. I think that you have your hands full, if you want to do jour job well.'

She walked a little closer to him. René always said that she had something of a lithe wild panther in her. A beautiful but dangerous animal. She needed an animal trainer, who could handle her. René thought that he was the one. This man next to her would do better….

'What do you do in your spare time?'

'Studying. Not only internal medicine, but also philosophy and so on. Life must be more than a successful career, a wife and children. What's the meaning of it? I look for that, and I look for it passionately. In my passion there's no

121

room for anything else.'

'Is that a rejection?'

He stood still and looked at her. His gaze went to the bone. This was a *man*! One had to conquer him, seduce him… she stared at the ground coquettishly with her beautiful brown eyes.

'We'll have a cup of coffee here.'

It sounded stern.

When she sat opposite him, he said:

'I didn't think about rejection, Agnes. You've had a boyfriend for years, haven't you?'

'Do you want to teach me a lesson in morality?' she asked, irritated.

He shook his head. Nietzsche was right. You did not have to be with Apollo, he is a boring fellow! Long live Dionysus!

He said rigidly:

'Certainly not. I just don't follow you. I told you what I keep busy with in my spare time, because you asked me. My answer had nothing to do with you. Nothing at all.'

She felt that she was blushing. This was a situation from a doctor's novel. Only there it all ended well after two hundred pages. This was real life. Was this man so innocent or was he playing a part? She was ashamed of her shame; *that* was real in any case. Shame for what? Because he saw through her, without meaning to. He just wanted to be friendly.

'Sorry.' she just said.

'It doesn't matter,' he said amenably and smiled at her.

The thing was, she felt that she had really fallen in love

with him. That should not happen, it made one weak and dependant. She liked the game of conquering, but she wanted to be in charge – and keep it that way.

At home that night, René, driven by his suspicion, said:
'Your mind is somewhere else, Agnes. What're you thinking about?'
'I'm tired, I had a night shift, remember?'
'You have night shifts all the time. This is different.'
'Stop prying! I'm tired.'
He thumped the table and got up.
'There will come a day when I shall give you a whipping!' he yelled angrily and walked off.
He had been saying that for years, over and over again. Because of that threat she had started going to karate class and now she knew exactly how to flatten someone out. She asked him once why he always threatened her but never really whipped her.
'I wouldn't forgive myself,' he had answered. 'Unless there was a real reason. Irritation or suspicion isn't a reason, is it?'
He was a good guy, René. He really loved her and she played with his love, she played with fire. But otherwise, there was no fun in it, nor much in her life. Asking yourself what the meaning of existence is was nothing to her. She gave sense to life by giving it some excitement. She loved lies and deceptions, the risk of being discovered. She did not get why one would fall into step. Why? She liked this beautiful blond Apollo and would do her best....

She became friends with him. She liked having lunch

with him and taking a walk with him afterwards, close to each other. He also liked her company; she did notice that. But he was unreachable, like Maria was unreachable for René. She could be his friend, but without one touch. He liked being around her, but there was not an iota of any physical attraction. She was on fire all the time, whereas he was quietly himself. She had a boyfriend, René, and was therefore just not available. When she knew him a little better, she asked him:

'If I weren't with René, would it be different between us?'

His answer surprised her.

'No. It wouldn't be different. Believe me, I'm not insensitive to women, really. But I believe in the saying of Goethe: that all transience is just a resemblance of the eternal. Woman is like that to me: the resemblance of a pure soul, pure thinking and feeling, altruistic desire. I strive after that in my own soul. I know that I can't search for that ideal outside myself.... Still, I don't see clearly how to handle that. In each case *the* woman for me... should *touch* me, completely. There shouldn't be anything abstract between us, no distance, actually no sex at all.'

'You're unreal!'

'Perhaps. Then let me be... until I can consciously enter that reality. Of course I could let myself go... I would for sure know how to do that but I don't want to. Not only because there is a René, but also because I just don't want to.'

'Do you understand anything about me?' she asked unhappily.

'Of course I understand something about you! You're a

124

pleasant friend, a close colleague. I like to talk to you, you are dedicated, an enthusiast.'

'But I'm too selfish. You want to say that too, don't you?'

'Ah, Agnes…. I believe that all people are driven by the same desire. Only their ways of seeking are different and have to be developed. I don't judge you.'

'You are too nice to judge me. Nevertheless, my way of living must be something incomprehensible to you.'

He shook his head.

'*I* am searching for a spiritual way out of unsatisfied desire. I want to understand, see through things. *You* search physically, in the excitement, in the touch.'

'You know that I'm not faithful. You must judge that, surely?'

He paused thoughtfully. She appreciated that he took her seriously, that he wanted to think about her. After a while, he said:

'I feel sorry for René. Very sorry.'

She sighed. For a moment she felt how *bad* it was. She cleared her throat and said:

'Well, he doesn't know about it. So it's not that bad.'

Something wonderful had happened to her. Her new friend was a true *friend*, someone who entered into discussion with her, someone who was truly interested in her. She felt a kind of love coming from him that softened her. She got used to the fact that there was nothing physical between them and had to accept it; it was something impossible. But because of that, her attitude towards René changed completely. Initially, her antipathy towards him grew to be almost unbearably strong. She blamed him that he was not like this young internist, so noble and quiet, so completely master of himself. Still, it was as if this antipathy came to a border where it turned around and came back as sympathy. She started to see René through the eyes of her friend – and started to long for more harmony in her contact with him. René was quite a nice guy to look at. Now they had a little more money, and he dressed how she liked him to. He was funny, even though there was always a certain sad intonation in his humour. He had a great knowledge of the human being, although she thought that it did not really have a deep basis. He was very musical, played the cello beautifully… and he was faithful and devoted. Because of that, because of all these good qualities, she was with him and stayed with him. Not out of fear of violence or something… but the two of them had developed bad habits in association with each other. They lived for themselves and met each other at home now and then. René was more in need of contact with her than she was and he was actually continuously angry and offended that she was always busy with something else. One wrong word or inconsiderate look could cause his bottled-up anger to explode into fury. His remorse over that usually meant they ended up in bed together, but even then he was not exactly a friendly lover. Now she had got to know such a completely different way of being with a man, her relationship with René seemed low and barbaric to her – she also knew that it was primarily her fault! The difficulty was that she was changing, while he stayed the same….

He usually came home earlier than she did and he prepared dinner then. What he made was always tasty and the dishes were always decorated beautifully. He did not have to do that for her, but suddenly she saw it now. She gave him a hug and said:

'Actually, you're a sweetheart, do you know that?'

Astonished, he looked at her and said:

'Why 'actually'?'

'It's quite bad that we live alongside each other. In my everlasting hurry I never see you anymore... not what you do, who you are.'

He looked at her seriously and asked:

'Have you never seen that, Agnes?'

She sighed.

'If you're always busy with yourself, you only see yourself.'

He pulled her against him and said:

'You only wake up from the dream of yourself when I kick or hit you – and afterwards I'm very much ashamed of that.'

Should she renounce her way of living? Become a devoted girlfriend, faithful to one man? Now that she and Johannes were friends, she could not possibly go on misbehaving. She would not be able to face him any longer.... Yet she loved the battle, the conquering, the secret life and the threat of being discovered. She was not created for a peaceful life. War it had to be, with the risk of being injured, the risk of death...

Quoting Goethe, René, who knew her so well, exclaimed:

'Oh, there are two souls within my breast!'

127

'Why did you stay with me, René? You aren't happy with it at all.'

'You're an addiction… because you don't give yourself to me. Never. You're absolutely on your own. That's also your power, your talent. But at the same time it's a flaw. I don't give up searching for you, my love.'

'You aren't really nice to me either. You are always tough, grim.'

He took her face in his hands. She could actually not handle that very well, he had to let her be. She was not his possession. But she controlled herself for once and let him do it. He said:

'It's my longing which has turned to stone, Agnes.'

'How should we change that, then?'

'Do you want to, Agnes? Do you want to change it?'

She nodded.

'Then let's start with *honesty*. There's an abyss between us, which is filled with unspoken feelings, thoughts, events. Unsolved conflicts. You have cheated on me, you don't know that I know that…. I've hated you for it, kicked you… I would sometimes want to kick you into the corner – but I want to find you…. In my work I see this all the time. There are people who become crazy from it, really insane. Perhaps we are both too *bad* to become crazy; we just go on living.'

She had the feeling that her heart had stopped; there was an unbearable pressure in her head, a congestion of heat. She felt that her face was red. She gasped for breath. What did he say? That he knew? Or did he mean something else? Was he talking about ordinary things?

128

He still held her face in his hands, because of which she really had to face him. What had she brought on herself in this moment of weakness?! He said:

'Honesty, Agnes. Without honesty there's nothing to change. You go your way, I go mine. I search for you and I don't find you. I'm very angry about that and I know that there'll come a time when I settle the bill with you, and your beautiful face will have to go against the wall in the end!'

She did not know what to say. It could be tactics, to force her to make a confession – and then settle the bill with her. That would be a physical settlement, like her cheating was physical too. A whipping or worse…. Or he did not know anything about it and was talking about the little things, the little lies, white lies or no white lies. It could also be that he was being really sincere and wanted to settle differences with her, now that she had asked for it herself. She looked at him, into his trusted eyes. There was a little yellow in his greyish eyes. She looked away and said:

'What do you mean, René? Be honest and tell me what you're talking about.'

He let go of her despondently. They had drifted too far apart. He did not even want to hear what she had to say. It should rather stay in the dark, untouched.

But she could not go back, nor forward anymore. She was nailed there, in the *present*. What had she done, for God's sake! If one lived a life like she did, one would never come to one's senses. *Never* ! Once that happened – and it had happened now – one could not move on anymore. And one could not go back. She had a paroxysm in her chest, most likely from hyperventilation. She felt stiff with fear, but she would tell him. Now. Like a jump from a ten metre high diving board. Just do it. And if it would break her neck – then it would just break it. Asking him again what he meant, was *weak*. She was weak, all lies are weak and all weak people are liars. A whipping or worse... what was the difference? It was something else if she would confess to it herself... or if he ever found out. What would Johannes say? Keep silent or speak? He only felt sorry for René. But if he already knew? Or didn't he? If he didn't, she was committing an accident now with her dive into the abyss.

'Come on, let's clear the table,' René said, turning away.

'Why, René?! Why are you ending the conversation? It's the first conversation in our relationship. Don't stop now!'

He turned towards her.

'I can't handle it. I know, but I don't want to know. Now it's still hidden in the dark.... Let me be, Agnes. Please.'

She started crying. She hated women who cried. Crying is weakness again. Fear of facing reality. She wanted him to pity her, so he would not get so angry with her. She had to say it now!

He started to clear the table. In the course of the years they had learned that. Clear the table immediately and put everything in the dishwasher. Let nothing lie around. They had a cleaning lady for the vacuum cleaning and washing the windows.

'Don't walk away now!' she yelled, stamping her feet.

He stood still, the plates, knives and forks in his hands.

'I warn you, Agnes. Shut up. I'll beat you to death if you

130

don't shut up.'

His eyes were yellow, full of hatred. She did not dare. She said:

'How can I ever be honest, if I'm not allowed to be honest? What changes about what you already know, if I say it openly?'

'It becomes reality then. That's what changes. Now I suffer from it, but then I'll have to take revenge.'

He is crazy, she thought. Really crazy. All psychiatrists are crazy. All surgeons are sadists. You should not be honest with someone crazy and a sadist does not let himself get beaten. Certainly not by someone crazy!

He took the dishes to the kitchen.

'I want to come to terms with myself and René, but it's not possible. If he hears what I've done, I'll get a whipping, or he'll strangle me or stab me to death with the kitchen knife. Or he'll hang himself, that's also a possibility.'

She relieved her feelings with her friend.

'What would you do, as a man… if you heard about something like that?'

He sighed.

'I don't believe it would get to that point. No, it wouldn't get to that point. Both of you have gone way too far; you are both to blame.'

'You're disgusted by it. And rightly so,' she noticed. 'Because of you, I can no longer live with it. I've never had problems with it before.'

'It's not my business.'

'Of course not. That's just the point. You're so objective

that I can see myself. I see myself and for the first time, I don't like what I see.'

She avoided René even more than before. She did not know how to behave anymore. She felt sorry for him and even more for herself. She did not want to make love with him anymore. His aggression became a horrible vision of murder and manslaughter. Still, she did not really believe it. There had to be a way out….

The only one who could help her was Maria. She had the purity which made René relax. Moreover, he still loved her very much. Perhaps she would know a way to bring them together.

Reluctantly, Maria accepted the mission to talk to René…. She did not feel like getting involved again in the lives of these two. On the other hand, she understood very well that the situation was somewhat dangerous – and that there was nobody who had more of a chance for successful mediation than her….

She welcomed René to her home, to her house in Limburg. Jean was at work, so she had the chance to talk to René quietly and for a long time. It was spring, the garden was in blossom, the apple tree had grown into quite a tree, with a blossom here and there….

They gave each other three friendly kisses and sat together a little uncomfortably at first. They never met alone anymore, and René was very tense. Suddenly he said:

'My sweet Maria… you've summoned me here, and I'm very nervous. It must be something very important!'

His nerves infected her. She had not prepared herself for this; she did not like doing it. The situation itself should point out the direction of the conversation. But now she had to deal with it.

'Agnes asked for it. She's totally out of it.'

He bowed his head and collapsed a little. She felt sorry for him. He kept silent. She hoped that the right words would come to her. She said:

'You know, René... Agnes has always led a wild life. She did already when she was a child. She's never had feelings of remorse. She lied easily and let me pay for her misbehaviour when it suited her. She had a lot of power, and I've always felt ugly and boring, the silly younger sister. Luckily, we had parents who saw through our relationship very well. But if we'd been born at the neighbour's house, I would often have had a whipping with the carpet-beater because of her wrongdoings. Of course we also had a lot of fun; she used to get up to the craziest things. But she lived for herself, sometimes ruthlessly.'

'You're speaking about the past,' René said lethargically. 'But it's still like that.'

'Look, René... I haven't understood why the two of you became a couple. I don't get it at all. You take her home one night... and from that moment on you are stuck on each other.'

'You are my love,' he said despondently.

'That isn't a reason to get involved with my twin sister. That's something impossible for her too.'

'It's not like that, Maria. She isn't a replacement. She's my fate, my destiny, if you want. My feelings for her are like a hurricane… I have no power to resist them. It's destructive, but lusty. You're too good for that, too good to understand something like that. If you two hadn't been sisters, things would've been exactly the same between us. I can't escape from her – and she can't escape from me.' Maria heard a little enthusiasm in his despondent voice.

'Right. It may be true. Certainly, I don't know any such restlessness. But now it's the way it is; now you're connected to each other, you must try to make something better of it.'

He doubled up.

'What do you think that I've been trying to do?!' He looked her in the eye now. 'I've been suffering because of that woman! Endless longing and experiencing that she is occupied with something other than me! With her profession, her friends, other guys, How should I know? With everything, except me! I keep her bound to me through frightening her with physical violence, giving her a foretaste now and then…. I have to tame her; with kindness I achieve nothing with her. Although I'd like to be kind, Maria, believe me. Just to be with her, like with you, is not possible. There has to be violence, passion. She is a panther, not a human being!'

'She's also a human being, you know that very well. But haven't you noticed a change, lately?'

'Yes I have. She avoids me even more and she doesn't want to be touched anymore.'

'She's afraid of you.'

'That's a good thing.'

'That's never a good thing. She's looking for a rapprochement, she wants to change. Haven't you seen that?'

134

'We talked, yes, a couple of weeks ago.' He collapsed again. 'Sometimes it's better to say nothing, Maria. How should I remain upright myself? I'd have to put on an act to find balance again. As long as I know nothing about it, I don't have to.

Maria was freezing. Here she was at the abyss of existence. Agnes had always escaped everything. Here she would be confronted with her behaviour, she had to leave – or let the abyss between her and René get bigger and bigger. What in God's name did she have to say? She said calmly:

'Listen, René. You've become a developed man, you are almost a psychiatrist, you know life and its complications. You should also be able to be a bit objective when it concerns your own life.'

'Yes.'

'When a patient comes to your practice who's in the same situation as you are now, what kind of advice do you give that patient then?'

He remained silent for a while. Than he said, his gaze fixed on the floor:

'I'd give him an anti-depressant, I would certainly do that. There is definitely a case of agitated depression, with a little paranoia probably – although that suspicion is certainly based in reality.'

'What should that man do to save his marriage?'

'I'm not married, but okay. He must talk – and keep his hands off her. Everything that has happened, is also his fault. He's not crazy, he knows very well what's going on. But he's too weak for a confrontation, too depressed, really. She gets a whipping now and then, she likes that – it mo-

135

tivates her to look around a little, pouting.' He looked up. 'He must talk, Maria. And listen. Just listen to what that bitch has been up to and then quietly separate, or forgive her. But he does not *want* that. He wants to beat her up; that's what he wants.'

'And then?'

'Become even more depressed, more silent – and feel again that she is cheating.'

'What do you think as a psychiatrist?'

He jumped up and shouted:

'That he's crazy! A psychopath, a sado-masochist! My God, Maria!'

She walked over to him and hugged him, like he was her brother. She felt how his body was tense, all defence. She caressed his hair and said softly:

'I'm so sorry for you, René.'

He relaxed somewhat.

'You can't help it. You know very well what she's up to and you're afraid that I'll kill her one day.'

'I'm also often very angry with her, René. Still, she's vulnerable, she's a very little girl actually – who wants to be important.'

'I know.' He was completely relaxed now. 'That touches me so much. If only I was able to be above it all. She should have someone who is above it.'

'*I* think that that someone must be you. You're much wiser than she is.'

'But as selfish as she is. That's the problem. I get hurt over and over again. Someone who is hurt, is not able to forgive.'

136

'Someone who doesn't ask for forgiveness, will not be forgiven. A beating is the one extreme, unasked-for forgiveness is the other. She has to understand what she's doing to you. Then your hurt would have a function, René.'

He sighed very deeply.

'What should I do now?'

'For me it would depend on how she acted. If you're able to have a conversation with her and you both want to stay together and she promises to do better, I would stay... otherwise I would leave. You'll have a lot of pain, but it'll pass – you know that.'

He sat down again.

'I hope that I can do it, Maria. She makes me so angry! Must she always get away with it?'

'You may be angry. If only you are *above* it. Damn it, you are not a child anymore!'

For the first time in the conversation, he smiled, and said: 'Wisdom... is a woman!'

Agnes had never been so nervous before.

René had left Friday morning to see Maria and would be coming home now, Saturday night. She had phoned him several times, but it was not answered. So she did not know a thing....

She watched a little television, walked around, washed the laundry and watched TV again.... She was frightened, depressed and yet full of expectation. She wanted to run away... she would certainly be confronted physically now. Maria....

A little after eight she heard the key in the lock. She jumped up and met him in the hallway. 'From fear - go for it!' her mother had always said.

He had changed, he seemed taller, tighter, more self-conscious. He looked at her for a while, walked past her, put up his coat and went into the living room.

'Would you like a cup of coffee?' she asked insecurely.

'Yes,' he said briefly and swung the door behind him. He sat where he always sat; it was the only thing that had remained the same. She put down the coffee and sat with him. Calmly, he took a packet of cigarettes from his pocket and lit one. He suddenly became a real man, not the restless boy anymore.... He took a long drag, sucked in the smoke deeply, blew it out again and looked at her.

'So,' he said. 'You've cheated on me many times.'

She felt shaken. She could react in the familiar way, bold and passionate... then her request to Maria would have been pointless. She could also feel the guilt, and the sorrow that she had caused this man. Strange, that one had a choice.... In the past she did not choose. She just *was*. Apparently, you entered another phase when you were over thirty. It was because of Johannes, because of his objective love.... While these thoughts crossed her mind, she felt uncomfortable that she had blushed. She bowed her head as a sign of confession.

René said:

'Well then. We must separate.'

She was flabbergasted. She had wanted to leave him so often and had not been able to, had not had the guts. Now he gave her the freedom and she was scared by it, she did not want it. Not anymore! She did not want to be sent

138

away, discarded. She was *Agnes*, a beautiful, interesting and intelligent woman! She jumped up and kneeled in front of him. She begged:

'No, René! Please... give me another chance!'

He was gauging her, she felt it. Was she faking, or was it for real? She was not sure herself. She just wanted to stay with him... that was real!

'It's one big lie, our whole life together! You've made me look like a fool, considered me an idiot who you can come home to while actually you're with someone else - '

His voice broke. She felt his closeness, that he was angry and at the same time broken. She had broken him and had not realized it. She had never thought of him, except when she was afraid of being discovered. Now she saw him sitting there, so controlled and strong – she had never thought that he could be like that. She was proud, but in her selfishness she did feel how much she was connected to this boy, who had suddenly grown up. She grabbed his hand and asked:

'Forgive me, René. Would you please forgive me? I didn't realize, I just did what I liked. It doesn't even have much to do with you. It's an endless longing for recognition, con-firmation. None of those men interested me like you do. I want to stay with you; I didn't know how well-off I was.'

He held her hand in his. Those fine hands of hers, which could do surgery so skilfully and make love so well. Was she sincere? He had no urge to hit her now. Perhaps he had to interpret that as a proof of her sincerity.... She lay at his feet like a child. He put his hand on her head and pressed it against his legs. He felt the value, the dignity of this moment. He gave her, the guilty one, forgiveness because she asked for it – because he could be above it.

She burst into tears. All the tension of the past weeks, months, years lived in her sorrow.

'I am so alone!' she whispered. 'So alone. Help me, René! Please stay with me!'

The solution of the problem of life is seen in the vanishing of the problem.

Ludwig Wittgenstein (1889-1951)

For several years the riddle of life was solved for Maria through love – or overwhelmed, made invisible. She married Jean, they lived in his house, had two children, a boy and a girl. When she was working, her mother was babysitting. Happiness saturated her whole existence and left no room for questions or dissatisfaction. Jean was a successful lawyer, but his desire to be with her was many times greater than his ambition. That made him plan his appointments during working hours. Evenings and weekends were reserved for his family.

Maria had always had a lot of comfort from beauty. Now the surrounding beauty was filled with the radiance of love too. Here a story could end, like a fairy tale....

She could talk with Jean for hours, they were always short of time. It was like they were two friends who had each other so much to tell after a long period of separation, that they could not stop talking. She loved the different sides of Jean. He was earnest and quiet, well-considered and a very demanding employer. But he loved travelling, nice food and 'beautiful' wine. He loved fast cars... and could give them up again just like that. He always looked good, whether he wore a grey suit and waistcoat, or a leath-

141

er jacket. At first he had great problems with Agnes and René; he felt that every visit was an agony. He could not stand Agnes' rashness and he thought that René was like a vagabond. But after the major changes in their relationship, it became better. He really made an effort to understand them and preach a little sense into them.

So it seemed that the problem of life and its meaning had disappeared for several years. The world, life as it presented itself to them was enough....

When the children went to school, they had more time again.... They always got up early, had breakfast with the four of them at the table, Jean went to work and she took the kids to school. At first there was a lot to do in the garden... but when the winter quiet set in, and it became colder, she was sitting in her house two mornings a week. She went to her parents, or into town now and then. She bought good books and read them. Often she was tired and rested a little. Should she work more? Jean was against it; she had less physical energy than he did....

For the first time in years it occurred to her that Advent was beginning. A wreath with four candles... in expectation of the birth of Jesus. Christmas.... *Empty* – that is how everything was. It was as if real life had moved into externalities, as if one could only find one's happiness in *things*. Internally, there was nothing left. Perhaps there had never been anything? The religious feelings from her childhood were perhaps also only experiences of *atmosphere*. The blessed atmosphere in church, her pious father beneath the apple tree. He was getting old… all the work was done by farm hands now. He was lean, with a weathered sunburnt face and a hat on his head when he went outside. But he was as bright as a fresh spring day. He seemed to become brighter and brighter. 'I know nothing', he always said politely, but on questions about life he always had unexpected, wise answers. If there was ever someone who lived internally more and more, it was her father. She would like to talk to him again like in the old days!

He was not sitting outside, for it was winter… he was in the kitchen, close to the stove, reading a book or listening to music – or he helped her mother with cleaning vegetables or folding the laundry.

'Hello, Maria child,' he said and looked at her searchingly with his blue eyes before he kissed her. She sat down with him.

'You've led a meditative life, dad. A life of contemplation, of prayer. How is it for you when you look at us, at your children? Who live so externally?'

The sun shone in his eyes. You always felt warmth and light when you were close to him. Smiling seriousness….

'You're busy,' he said. 'Agnes has her career; you give the example of a good marriage, of a beautiful family. I feel deep satisfaction, Maria.'

'Of course. You wouldn't say anything else. But we aren't exactly following in your footsteps, are we?'

He shook his head.

'Not Agnes. But *you* are, child.'

'I think life is so superficial. It's almost Christmas now, I grew up with it and now it's nothing to me. It is something, but I *experience* nothing anymore. I still believe in it, but I'm never occupied by it. Does an inner life even exist? I wonder at such moments. But you *have* it, at least, so it seems.'

'Do you want me to tell you about the inner life?'

'Yes, if you want to.'

He leaned forward a little. An old farmer on a chair in the kitchen near the stove. That was the outer image, it was a *disguise*....

'My inner life, child... exists in dwelling. I'm not familiar with haste, which is so familiar to you. I don't live *past* life, but I live *with* it, dive into it and... dwell upon it as long as possible. On the positive, if possible. One could have a lot of grief over a daughter like Agnes, and could decide to live *past* it. I don't want that. I see her and later on, she has an after-effect on me... her energy, her lust for life, her ambition. I don't only have that with people, but also with clouds, with the morning sun, and nightfall, with the warmth of the fireplace... I thank the Lord that He is here among us and gives us these *experiences*... the happiness of the experience, child, is something divine. I take life as it is, but I dive into it and carry it with me. Respect for everything around me – and gratitude for the experience... my inner life consists of that. I've worked with pleasure, because I loved everything, my trees, my farm hand, my wife and children... this wooden table on the scrubbed floor. The smell of beeswax and soap.... You have no time for that, you don't come around to it, everything has to be done quickly....'

144

'I think that I have too much time at the moment. Because of that I feel an emptiness that I can hardly bear. So you say: dwelling on your experiences?'

He nodded, but then said:

'Only I'm afraid that it doesn't count for you anymore, that it's no longer possible to do that. You've learned to be busy with your intellect all day – and that's not suited for experiences. I'm not familiar with it, that intellectual thing. But I see in you how it works, effects. You become global through it, a little summarizing and swift analyzing. Things are like this, like that and so it's done with! So René won't find wisdom with all his philosophy and Agnes with all her knowledge about anatomy won't have any real knowledge of the human being. It's not possible. Those little ones of yours are starting to reason already, they have to. And you answer their elementary questions with your grown-up intellect – they become smart alecks with it. In the past one got a beating for that, so one learned to be silent.'

'We never had that. I could never do that.'

He smiled.

'Nor could I. You can't train such a holy thing as a child like a dog. But in the past it was like that and it did teach you humility. Today an infant already thinks that he is allowed to have his own opinion.'

'So you do see the negative side?'

'That's inevitable – and the experience of it causes *suffering*. I seek reality, not a seventh heaven. But where I have the choice, I fix my eye on the positive.'

'But you don't think that it'll work for me?'

'You'll have to *seek* your path, child. You have a high inner development, I'm sure of that. Ask yourself questions and you will find the answers, sooner or later. For the Lord is among us. He answers all your questions – if you ask.'

That night she sat together with Jean by the burning fireplace. She drank a glass of red wine. She looked at him. He was the kind of man who woman fell in love with easily, but he was absolutely not interested in them. His whole capacity for love was concentrated on her... and he made her warm and happy. Of course there was disagreement sometimes. They had completely different points of view on certain things. He liked to live generously, while she was used to being economical and to simplicity. She indeed liked to be pampered, but sometimes it was too much.... So there were small things on which they did not agree.

'What are you looking at!' Jean said shyly.

'I'm counting my blessings,' she smiled. 'This afternoon I was with daddy; we spoke to each other very deeply again.'

'About what?'

'About... happiness and dissatisfaction. I'm blissfully happy with you and the children – and nevertheless feel increasing dissatisfaction.'

He nodded and filled a pipe with tobacco. He said:

'You have work that's beneath your quality.'

'That might be good. Otherwise that consciousness of a deep longing for... more, for something internal, for religion, would never arise. One can fill one's life with working and caring, but it isn't only about that, is it? Have you multiplied your talents? That will be the final question before or after death. I don't think that I'm busy with that. I have

146

rather lost what I used to have.'

'It lives in our love, Maria.'

'Yes. I don't want to diminish that love, or underestimate the value of it. It's just the satisfaction it gives, the saturation of it, which gives me the opportunity to feel the absence of 'that other'. At first, I had thought that I was lacking a man. That was right, at that time. I know that I started *living* after I met you. In *life* I can't imagine anything more beautiful or better than moments like these, now. Still, this sitting by the fireplace with my lover wouldn't have such value, if there was only a physical harmony. I feel the relation to my own way of living: only a physical satisfaction, a good relationship, but no intensification. One never gets beyond the surface of things, even if they are very beautiful....'

He leaned backwards and pulled on his pipe.

'What did your father say?' he asked.

'That he *dwells* on his experiences. That dwelling on them brings him in contact with the being of things and man – I believe even with the being of the divine. But we don't know how it has to be done, do we? *Dwelling...* what is that?'

'Love is our teacher, Maria. I don't know a lot about the being of things, but all the more about your being – because I love you. Your father must have that love on a higher and more extensive level. He is *good* through and through. The complete cosmos is reflected in him, because he surrenders without any defence. We aren't able to do that, but perhaps it can be learned. You'd like to have a greater inner peace, in which life can sow its seeds. When you look at your father, you'd say: the first step is respect, awe. Think about his eyes, how they look into the world... that's devotion, Maria. I have that for you, I adore you. But I agree with you: one should be like that with everything in life: your client, your colleague... everything and everyone.'

'You must obviously be on guard in your profession. But beyond that it would be right. How do you come to that idea?'

'Through your father, as I told you. He's devotion itself... his whole *being* is prayer.'

'Something like that would have to become an exercise in our case. Daily life makes it hard to manage that.'

'I've read about it, in the past. I don't remember where it was.'

She shivered, despite the warmth of the fire.

'Are you cold?' Jean asked.

'No. Sometimes I have the feeling of being touched; that makes me shiver. Not physically, but from the inside. As if I'm enlightened for a short while, but the light hurts. Then I think that I'm going to faint, but it doesn't happen.'

Jean sat up straight and put his pipe on the table. He looked at her and said seriously:

'Maria, if there is a God, it seems to me that He's connected to the good part in every human soul. If that goodness is very big, there's a big connection. That God would want to reveal Himself to these people if they are looking for Him. You are someone like who's looking.'

'Do you think that I'm looking for Him? Is that my desire?'

'I do think about such questions of yours, Maria.'

148

'What remains of us after death?' she asked her father. He did not hesitate for a moment and answered:

'The moral value of what we've done, felt and thought. The rest has to fall away. The more *good* we've done, the more remains of us. Our evil part remains exiled around earth, or, if you wish: thrown into hell.'

'I've always thought that was very harsh, pitiless.'

Father shook his head.

'The divine world, 'heaven' only takes in what's connected to it. The rest is rejected. It must wait for transformation outside Heaven's door.'

'How will it be transformed? By whom?'

'By man himself, in a new life on earth.'

'Do you believe in that? In reincarnation?' she exclaimed, astonished. Her father, who went to Holy Mass devotedly every Sunday and went to communion...

Her father bowed his head and said softly:

'I've had to fight a lot, child, with the dogmas of the Church and my own inner experiences. Sometimes I have explanations in the night, a clarity in my sleep... then I know about it, I feel the moral judgement on my deeds, I remember a life before birth. There's not only immortality, but also unbornness. Still, I want to be one of the sheep of the Good Shepherd. The Church is the shepherd; I have to adjust – and feel insights inside me that are so different!'

A simple farmer at a sanded kitchen table by the burning stove, her father. So quiet on the surface.... Again she felt that intense painful light for a moment, that made her dizzy. She shivered and said:

'Jean lately said the same, but then the other way around.

149

That a good human being has such a connection to the divine that God unites with his or her soul. As heaven takes in the pure human part, so the pure human part takes in the divine. What you are given of insights must be of such a nature. I can't see sin in that!'

'You were brought up free, sweet child. I was not. And one should always remain very critical, believe me. Overestimation of oneself is much closer than the notion of sin.'

'Neither seem good to me,' Maria said as she took her father's weathered hands in hers and caressed them. 'To me you are indeed the living proof that there's an invisible, inner reality beside the tangible reality....'

When she visited her parents one morning, an old man was sitting with her father at the kitchen table. When he saw her, he looked up, but his hollow glance lingered on her without recognition. She recognized him, albeit with difficulty. It was the neighbour, farmer Erens. He looked like he was ninety years old, crooked and weathered, vacant. Creaking he got up, shook her father's hand and with a furtive glance at her, made his way out.

'He looks bad!' she said, as she sat down.

'He is declining. He tells endless stories about the past, but doesn't know what is going on in the present. His spirit is buried in his body, child. There's no balance in that man, he's vegetating a little until his body becomes exhausted. His spirit will be released then, but with strain, I'm afraid.'

'Do you really *see* that, dad? Or do you believe that that's what you see?'

'I see it. But not with my eyes, although they help in for-

150

ming a whole picture. When I look at your mother, I see how her spirit is becoming more and more free. But Erens is buried in Erens. I hope that he's had enough faith to find his way up.'

'He was always sitting in the front row at Church, with all his children?'

'That might also be show, right. Ah... Erens is not a bad man, you know that.'

'I was always very afraid of him. That he would grab me and spank me.'

'He had respect for you, child. He still talks of you with regard. You didn't have to be afraid.'

She thought about her childhood with melancholy. It had been soaked in a mood of comforting holiness. Now everything had become profane, sober reality. The world is not a mystical riddle, but an understandable piece of machinery. Not that she believed that, but she lived it; there was nothing else. Even the apple tree did not have that wonderful effect that it still had a couple of years ago....

'Everything you have inside comes from the senses,' she sighed that evening for the hundredth time to Jean.

'How can you release yourself from that? It can't be anything else than an imprisonment in the body? Today I saw in farmer Erens where that leads to. Daddy says: *Experience* what you gain from your senses. The experience is *not* physical. But I'm certainly not able to experience it. Also, wonder is short-lived. I can do it for a short time, but then sense takes control and the mood's gone. Why can't I just be satisfied with what is there, like everybody else?'

151

'And those little 'enlightenments' that you often have?'

'They're more frightening than merciful. I'm shocked by them, shaken to my core. If they became stronger, I'd be overcome by them. And I don't know what they are.'

'Epiphany.'

She kept silent. Jean could make overly dramatic remarks, from his love and understanding for her. But she thought that his image of her was too grand....

*

After the crucial night, when René had come to Maria, a tough time started for Agnes. René expected her to prove to him that their relationship meant very much to her. He wanted to give her a chance for another six months. To her it was a sort of exam. She had no problems stopping trying to seduce other man. Her love for her friend Johannes had already ended that. But to focus completely on René in her life was difficult for her. She had always been the mighty one, and he the desperate lover. He had restrained her with the threat of violence, but she knew his passionate love for her very well. Now the roles were reversed; it had happened in one night. The awareness that she lost him had proved to her how much she loved him. But to lie at his feet night after night.... He had changed completely. Boys like him, a little fragile and petty, mostly become better with the years. They gain dignity and weight; he was becoming an attractive man. But that one night had also made him confident. He was suddenly above her and made her feel it. He was a lot nicer than before, even kind. He used to fight with his hands and feet and walk away after that. Now he became a *gentleman* when he was angry, a gentleman who only had to warn her. She was a sinner, who indeed got mercy, but still had to prove that she was worth it. That role was nothing for her, but nevertheless, she took it on. She went with him to his concerts and horse riding. He visited her lectures for colleagues and then parties with them. Her life became completely interlaced with his. She got to know him better: his interests, his friends, his questions, his love for her. She thought it was all very limited, that she had to focus her whole enthusiasm on this one person, René. It was not completely like that... she had her job, the patients, the colleagues, Johannes at lunch... but one way or another, she felt it humiliating to have to give all her spare time to René now. She was at his feet, like that one night. She wanted it, she did not want it.

When he had finished his specialisation, he got a job in The Hague. With great reluctance, she followed him. She had to do the last two years of her specialisation in Leiden, say goodbye to her friends, to Johannes. In return, René asked her to marry him. They bought a dignified house in one of the long, light streets of The Hague. He had a practice at home, beside the office hours at the hospital. René was the big shot, the important specialist. She was his wife and outside the spotlight, she finished her specialisation to become a surgeon, which wasn't much either.... All the glory of the old days was gone; she was just a nice pretty

153

young woman, married to a good psychiatrist. At the clinic she had to start over as well. Nobody knew her qualities, she missed the combativeness she had before and was a common assistant, neither a good one nor a bad one. She put on a little weight, here and there amongst all her black hair a grey hair or two appeared, which she would pull out fiercely. For every grey hair that she pulled out, ten came in return…. At night she brought René fresh coffee, when he was studying at the long table in his library. If she wanted, she could join him….

'May I say something?' she asked on one of those nights.

She sat opposite him at the table. Her journals were on it too; she browsed through them, dispirited. René looked up, slightly disturbed.

'Yes?'

'Are you happy now with your good wife? Have I passed the exam?'

He burst into a laugh. He reached over the table and clapped on her cheek.

'Are you still busy with the exam?' he asked.

'Yes.'

'Perhaps it should stay like that. Otherwise you'll become careless again.'

'You've become a real lad. Where's that boy I used to know?'

'Here,' he said. 'Opposite you. Through sorrow he grew into a man. This is the way he is now, do you understand?'

'Is the sorrow over now, René? she asked softly.

He sighed deep and pushed his book aside. She loved the man that he had become, but still missed the boy. She had neglected that boy so much, and now he was gone. He looked at her and said:

'It'll never go away. And the confidence is not a hundred percent yet.'

She begged:

'What do I have to do to make it up to you? I do everything that you want me to. You've become stern, distant. Kind, but so unreachable. It's a continuous punishment that's already lasted for years....'

'That's not my intention, Agnes. Because of what happened I've developed myself in a positive way, I think. I've become much stronger and more certain. It wasn't my intention that it would be at your expense. I love you very much, you do know that, don't you?'

'You've accepted this sinner mercifully. I have to feel that, every day.'

'Not at all. The first time maybe, but not anymore.'

'You say it yourself, that you don't completely trust me yet. That hurts, René. I've given up everything, I did so years ago already. For the sake of our relationship.'

He got up and came to her. They had been living together for thirteen years now and he had managed to make her fall in love with him again completely, just by not giving himself to her completely anymore.... She also got up and laid herself in his arms. He had cast her off, even though he had forgiven her and kept her with him. Now she was allowed to be there again, she was home again. Warm, salty tears were streaming down her cheeks, without sniffing. His coat became wet.

'Come to me,' he whispered, touched. 'Come... you're

sweet. I admire you for the ability to change. We psychiatrists don't believe that's possible. I do, because I've seen it with you. I've never meant to torment you, I thought that you were satisfied.'

He lifted her head and kissed her tenderly, like he had never done before.

She completely surrendered and cried until she was completely exhausted.

Well, she had not become a *good* woman at once. With René it was good, he knew how to handle her. But her bad characteristics sought a way to express themselves. She thought that goodness made one *weak*. One has to take all kinds of factors beyond oneself into account that held up one's own development. When she had been free from René, she was able to do whatever she wanted. Now she *wanted* to be with him, but she also had to keep his interests in balance with hers. Her ambition blossomed again. She had fine, feminine hands that did their job extremely fast and accurately. Naturally that was noticed, and more and more often the professor wanted to have her next to him during surgery. She also kept her knowledge up to date and so never dropped a stitch. She liked to be an embodiment of authority and was a difficult tutor to the young assistants and interns. She had a nose for those who were timid, took them pitilessly by the scruff of their necks and threw them in the deep end. Anxious doctors are *bad* doctors, was her motto. She avoided every form of friendliness and enjoyed her power, which she afterwards gladly relinquished when it became a question of retaining the favour of the professor. Thus it came to the carefully prepared moment when she was asked by the professor to stay on after her studies. She could promote and work in scientific education.

But at home, at The Hague, there was a different plan for the future. René was a respected specialist who went to a lot of parties, a reception here, a dinner there. Agnes' future was quickly arranged: she could get a spot in one of the corporations after her study. A woman in the team would be an interesting replacement ...

She was much more interested in a career in Leiden. There was still a chance that she would reach the top because there was also a demand for female professors. This was what she wanted, but how could she persuade René? She thought she should just throw it at him like a projectile....

'René, I can stay in the clinic when I'm finished. Get a promotion, give lectures ... it seems fantastic to me.'

She saw that he was startled. He blushed a little and said: 'But... you were going to...'

'That was your idea. And financially, this is definitely more attractive, you know that. You can see how it has been for Johannes. He has also remained at the clinic, is head of the clinic now, and everybody knows that he's going to become professor when this one leaves.'

'Johannes is a different case. He devotes his whole *being* to the profession. You have other responsibilities. I thought that we'd agreed on that at this point. You're thirty-four years old. I'd like to have a couple of children.'

She sighed. Children, my God! He kept on talking about

children… she did not want to be a mammal, intended for reproduction.

'We could have a dog.' she said.

'Agnes!' René said fiercely. The gentleman got angry and called her to order.

'And?' she asked challenging.

'Would you compare a child to a dog?'

'Why not? They are affectionate, one has to potty-train them and teach them to be obedient. What is the difference?'

Of course she knew but she just wanted to nag. Before, he would have hit her; now he distanced himself. He said sternly:

'Agnes, stop it. You just want to have it your own way and are trying to shock me. We're both familiar with that now. You've put yourself in the centre enough, right?'

'Why do you always have to bring that up again? I've made myself small enough. You've made me feel what I did to you for several years and now that I'm starting to grow a little, I'm not allowed to.'

'You can still leave. Than you can grow beyond yourself and choke all the rest as far as I'm concerned. But not next to me, not anymore!'

'So you won't allow me to make my own career?' she asked fiercely.

'It's not a matter of not allowing; that's nonsense. Such a career is not possible in our lives, Agnes. Be realistic. You want to shape reality your own way, instead of fitting in.'

'Then there's no freedom. To me freedom means forcing circumstances to conform to your own wishes.'

'And the wishes of others?'

'It's the law of the strongest.'

He got up. He was high above her. He said:

'*I* am the strongest, Agnes. If you're staying with me, you're not going to Leiden.'

She hated him at such moments. But at the same time she felt her love in that hate. She loved this dolt, damn it! And just because he affirmed himself as the strongest.

'So it's a prohibition,' she claimed, stubbornly.

'Look here, Agnes,' he said, with all the patience he could muster. 'Apparently, it's necessary that I remind you over and over again of the pact that we've made. If our relationship means anything to you, you'll make sure that you have the time for it. As a surgeon you'll be busy enough and you will of course be an important lady then too. I love you and I want to see you in my children. 'He bowed and kissed her on the lips. Electricity went through her body. She shivered.

He pulled her up.

'You're just a naughty child,' he grinned. 'Come with me, I'll make you feel who is the strongest!'

'Love makes you weak,' she said to Maria.

They were walking on the beach. They did not see each other alone often; the men were always with them and often Maria's children too.

'What nonsense,' said Maria. 'Love is for the strong. They give what they have extra to the weaker ones.'

'That makes me even sicker!' yelled Agnes. She walked deliberately into the wind, her head held up high, the wind in her hair. 'Everyone for himself, please!'

'What do you mean by 'love'? Why does it make you weak?'

'I want to develop without restraints, Maria!' she yelled above the wind. 'In that, there's no place for love!'

'That's like only wanting to breathe out. Then you'll die. There's always something coming towards us that modifies our possibilities.'

'I hate that! It goes against freedom! René limits me, because I love him.' She stood still and said softly: 'I truly love him. Who would ever have thought that? I'm expecting, Maria!'

Maria's eyes grew large with astonishment.

'You?'

'Yes, me.'

'How is that going to work?'

'Pregnancy leave and then the baby in the crèche.'

They walked on.

'It feels unbelievably good, Maria, this new life in my body, I would never have thought it. It seemed more like a humiliation, to grow something that comes from such a guy. But it's given me vitality and self-reflection at the same time. I've been reflecting on the phenomenon of freedom. Who has the power, man or the existing reality?'

'So you're not staying in Leiden?'

'René won't let me. To confirm that, he's given me a child as a chip on my shoulder.'

Maria had to laugh. Agnes was a crazy woman!

'It didn't happen without your consent, I believe.'

Agnes stood still again and grabbed her sister's hand. She beamed.

160

'I love life, Maria!' she cried. 'But… does freedom exist too?'

'You live in paradoxes.' Maria said, as they walked on hand in hand. 'You want freedom and you love it that you have a man who lays down the law for you. You hate love and sing it at the top of your voice. Having a child is a humiliation and the most beautiful thing there is. You think that I'm a dullard with my husband and children and my poor little job….'

'You are my idol!'

Maria, moved, felt her sister, who was not an hour older than she was, hopping like a child next to her – that was a paradox too.

Nothing is, therefore, the same determination,
or rather absence of determination,
and thus altogether the same as, pure *being.*

G.W.F. Hegel (1770-1831)

She sat underneath an old apple tree on a bench. The knotty old tree spread its leaves broadly, forming a roof above her.

She was almost forty years old, and she had buried her father in this graveyard yesterday. It smelled sweet here, like it had also smelled at home, in the bedroom where they had laid out his body. A small, weathered man with a spirit as great as the universe....

It had all happened very quickly; his death had caught them off guard. There had been nothing by which one could have felt the end approaching. She had sat next to him on their trusty spot only a week ago. He had revealed more and more of his spiritual secrets to her, as if he wanted to bequeath to her all his knowledge. But he was fresh and cheerful as always. The day after, he got a fever and started coughing. Antibiotics did not work; it had to be a virus. But he became more and more depressed and dull. They did not manage to keep him alive in the hospital. After only three days he died....

She had been even more startled by Agnes' reaction. Agnes was desperate, in a panic even. She had screamed... she

163

had had so much to ask him, which she had put off – he was still young, not yet seventy. She had wanted to settle her differences with him, her father. She was distraught, inconsolable; she did not stop crying. They had all tried to calm her down and convince her that he had not become *nothing*, that he was still there, even though no longer tangibly. But her materialism was not shallow. For her, if something was no longer tangible, it no longer existed. That made her grief unbearable, not only to herself, but also to those around her.

Maria had watched by him, by that little weathered body around which his great spirit floated. She could not understand how Agnes did not see that. To Maria, it was a certainty, a fact. She had read from the New Testament while sitting next to him. Agnes had come in once very quickly, and fled again. She could not handle the confrontation with that spiritless body, even though she had experienced the dying of others so often in her work.

Mom was very strong in her deep sorrow. Across death, she felt the connection with the man with whom she had lived for decades bound in unity. Nothing could part her from him. She caught Agnes in her arms, kept her grandchildren busy and was the spindle everything turned around. While Maria sat with the body, Jean took care of the funeral... and René had his hands full with Agnes.

It did not pass. During Holy Mass Agnes' distraught sobbing was heard continuously; she did not go to the graveyard and sat pale and tiny in a corner at coffee; she could not understand how all the family members and acquaintances could go on talking and laughing. That had been yesterday. Now Maria was sitting alone on a bench at the graveyard. Oh, she missed him too... she would keep missing him. The sadness and longing were like a heavy veil over her eyes, around her shoulders. But through that veil she felt the glory of her father. For him it was accomplished, this life on earth. He could observe his Lord now, as he had worshipped Him during his life. Here on earth he had felt the world of the angels and archangels so strongly... now he had come home, after a long, productive journey. That certainty made her sadness bearable....

'Maria.'

She was startled from her contemplations and looked up, tears in her eyes. A tall, unknown man stood before her. No, not unknown... vaguely known.

She got up and shook his hand.

'Johannes Leven,' he said.

'Ah... Professor Leven. I've heard about you from Agnes.'

He smiled.

'And I've heard about you. Do you mind if I call you by your first name?'

'Of course not,' she sighed. 'I know you very well from her stories. Is it a coincidence, that we meet each other here?'

'Yes and no. I came to the funeral for Agnes' sake. We're staying with my parents; they live nearby. I wanted to come back today to... experience your father once more. I didn't know him, but his funeral was revealing.'

'Agnes is inconsolable. We don't know what to do with her.'

He was silent. They walked to the grave. She had heard a lot about this man, about his way of life, his promotion, his becoming a professor, his marriage to a student. Agnes had been there all the time... he was a friend of her sister, of whom she was very proud. Now they were walking here, to her father's grave, as if they knew each other very well. She immediately felt something very familiar.

They stood still by the freshly dug grave, which was studded with bouquets already withering.

The light, which struck her so painfully, joined with those withering flowers. It came from them, was one with them. It was deprivation of the most intense kind... she staggered, Johannes took her by the arm and supported her.

'Careful,' he said.

Ah... in the light of deprivation, she felt her father. She felt his holiness, completely free now.

'What was your father like?' Johannes asked, while still supporting her.

She looked at the grave, at the withering flowers.

'He was a holy man,' she said quietly. 'One of those men who live a great life in simplicity, a blessing to all around him, but also to a greater whole – even though he hardly left his birthplace. His life was a prayer... he treated everyone and everything with respect. Still, you're not aware enough of that... you know that a miracle is among you, and you realize it only when it's become invisible. That's Agnes' despair too, remorse for her neglect of what was possible, for the nonchalance in which we live. And she's afraid of her own end.'

They were silent. Here she was at her father's grave. And she herself? Was she afraid of her own end? There was that unbearable light of deprivation, that was also a consolation.... In waves it came and went through her, like her sorrow had freed itself from her and had become something independent that came back to her as light. Again she staggered.

'What's wrong?' the man beside her asked, while he held her steady. 'Are you all right?'

'I have this more often. My husband says that it's God, who wants to reveal Himself to me. It hurts.... And makes me happy at the same time.'

That she could say something like this to a stranger, who was yet so familiar to her....

'Perhaps you'd rather be alone?' he asked her carefully.

'No, no. I'm happy that you are here. It's been a long time.'

It has been a long time... for a lifetime you aim your steps towards a certain moment, a great meeting. Suddenly the moment is there... and must be *realised*. What her father had meant to her, had reappeared, in a new form, next to her....

She felt weak on her legs, light in her head. But she did see him very distinctly, she felt his physical support. She always saw everything very clearly and detailed. Colours, shapes, beauty.... If you would only *look*, you would call this man handsome, an attractive man in his forties. Tall, thick blond hair, beautiful blue eyes, laughter lines. But with him she 'saw' something else too. With him you could not stop at his physical appearance. It was something like the difference between a photograph and the living reality. She had never met someone before who had living reality around him, with him so much. If you did not believe in the spirit, a meeting with this man would make your conviction shake. Because this was no sensory observation, she could distinguish that very well from the other; it was so very present. Because of this, she just felt a very strong connection, as if the staggering was an understanding of it. Everything that is in the inside comes from the senses, she had always thought. But this? She was sure of the non-sensory character of her observation.

'Do you want to go home? Shall I take you?' he asked.
She shook her head.
'No… I want to go back to that bench beneath the apple tree for a while.'
He took her there, but stayed with her. He sat next to her.
'Dying is a peak in our existence,' she said. 'These three days have been the most elevated days I have ever experienced, in spite of the grief. I've always believed in a spiritual life before and after life on earth, but now it's become a reality. The silence of my father's body was in such a contrast with the liveliness of his spirit around it… can one perceive something like that in a living human being?'
He was dwelling deeply on her question, she also observed that. He did not just listen, but was really immersed in

what she said. He replied:

'Then there must be a large free part, a free spirit. One that isn't completely buried in the body.'

'How does one come to that? Die a little, before dying...?'

'You must search for what in yourself naturally has the most affinity with death, what *is* even dead. In that the forces of arising slumber, but they *slumber*. They want to be awakened; they want to leave you free to want it yourself. They can send their heralds, to tell you that they are there. That's happening to you now... they're threshold experiences, conditions of powerlessness. You are brought to the threshold of your body, but your consciousness is too strong to persist outside your body.'

'But that dead part inside you... what do you mean by that? It sounds terrifying. One normally thinks that one is completely *alive*.'

Again, she felt that he was deep in thought. He said:

'Once there was a man who asked me: What is your greatest ability? I had to answer: My ability to understand, to see through connections.

His next question, however, was: What is your greatest obstacle? I had to answer almost the same. I said: My brains. Because I experience everything at a great distance because of them.

Then he asked again: What is the greatest riddle? I answered: Dying.

His next question was: What touches you the most? I said: Saying goodbye.

Then I was given a task, Maria... the greatest one in my life: 'Search, with your greatest talent, for the origin of what touches you the most. Then you will fathom the riddle and overcome your obstacle.'

She was deeply touched, even though she could not directly follow the meaning. She asked:

'Why does someone talk in such riddles, so disguised? Why doesn't he just say what he means?'

'It was so deep, Maria... something like that shouldn't be expressed in sober language; it would lose all its effectiveness, its power.'

'Did you understand what he meant?'

'At the moment itself, there was a feeling of complete understanding, but it was undifferentiated. Later, at home, I went over his words in my mind and my feelings, meditated on them... and understood the sense of them, the task.'

She felt that she could not ask him to explain that *sense* soberly now. She asked:

'Would you please repeat his questions and your answers again?'

She listened and took his words in so intensely that she would be able to repeat them later, at home....

He took her to the farm in his car. She said:

'Will we see each other again?'

'Whenever you want.'

'If you're still here tomorrow, come for a coffee with your wife. We'll be staying here for a couple more days, with my mother. Agnes is there too.'

She felt his reserve. He said:

'I'd rather speak to you alone once more.'

'Tomorrow at the graveyard then? Twelve o'clock?'

'OK,' he said. He helped her get out of the car and waited until she walked up the property. She heard the engine starting and the car driving away.

'Where the hell have you been?' Jean strode around angrily. 'I've been very worried! You went to the grave 'for a moment'. For a moment! You've been away for two hours!'

'Sorry,' she said calmly. 'I didn't feel well and met Johannes Leven, Agnes' professor. He stayed with me until I felt better and took me home.'

'I don't like that at all!' he yelled angrily. 'They should leave you alone, those sorts of friends of Agnes!'

'Don't act like a fool, Jean! I'm meeting him again tomorrow. He's a very profound man.'

'Oh, I'm sure he is! Charming a woman when she's vulnerable!'

She started to get angry too now.

'What's wrong with you?' she shouted, as she walked inside.

He came after her, grabbed her arm and forced her to stand still. Furious, she hit him in the face with her other hand and was shocked by it herself. He turned her around with a pull and hit her hard on her back. She became wild and started to defend herself fiercely.

'What *is* this? Stop it, you two!'

Agnes had walked into the hallway and was looking at the fighting couple, astonished. Maria and Jean - the perfect pair!

Panting, they let go of each other. Maria burst into tears. He had become *mad* ! Her father had died, had just been

171

buried, she had become unwell, and Jean suddenly became jealous. What was happening to him? What was this?

Jean took her into his arms.

'I'm sorry, love, sorry! I was mad with fear! I am sorry!'

She pushed him away.

'I've had enough of you,' she said sobbing. 'I don't understand this at all.' She turned around and walked towards the stairs. 'I'm going to lie down.'

Jean walked with her and stood there awkwardly while she undressed. He had a red cheek and she felt burning spots on her body. It was ridiculous. They had never fought like that. She looked at him and said:

'What *is* this, Jean? What's happened to us?'

He came to her and hugged her.

'We're tired, a little exhausted. Come on, we'll forget it. You're going to him tomorrow, I trust you a hundred percent. Lie down, and tell me what he's told you.'

Sobbing like a child, she got into bed and told him about the meeting with Johannes Leven.

When he had gone downstairs, she tried to remember the conversation with Johannes. But now, she was too confused to remember the sentences clearly. Nevertheless they were crucial, those sentences. It seemed almost as if the incident had been staged to erase her memory of them completely. Her father used to say: Everything in life aims to bury you in matter, remember that, child. The senses give an image of Gods greatest creation, but they also seduce you and capture you in the transient part of it. To release yourself from the power of the senses is like performing a miracle:

you break through the necessity of natural law. But believe me, child: one moment of release leads to many hours of heavy battle with the forces that want to take it away from you again. There will come a time when you will experience that painfully. Think about what I always told you then, my dear Maria.'

She also felt it that way... this did not have much to do with the essentials between her and Jean, but it did have to do something with Johannes. The meeting with him was apparently of the greatest interest....

He was waiting for her beneath the apple tree in the graveyard. She was a little late, because everything seemed to obstruct her leaving the house. Jean had a bad temper, the children held her up with their nagging, and Agnes was curious about where she was going....

He was a gentleman, an old-fashioned professor... but at the same time young and energetic. He seemed to be sunk in meditation, his hands folded, the head bent a little. But he got up immediately when she approached him. They shook hands. He was a stranger naturally... and still... she expected a lot from this conversation.

'Do you want to take a walk or sit here?' he asked.

She wanted to take a walk, into the hills, her father's land.

'Sit here,' she said, thinking about Jean's warnings.

'I remember you,' he said, looking into the distance. 'The physiology practicum, where I was an assistant, and you were a quiet, shy girl. Do you remember?'

It was as if lightning struck her heart. The boy who had

been her ideal. Jean looked nothing like him…. But he had changed so much, then!

'Are you him?' she asked with a trembling voice. 'You used to be such a… sunny, cheerful boy – and now you're such a serious man. Is that *you*?'

He still looked into the distance.

'A lot has happened since then. I've become a scholar. It was the only thing in which I became aware of *spirit*, albeit abstract, thin, schematic. I've given my whole energy, Maria, my youth, my *everything* to the development of my thinking. I did it from an unrestrained desire for insight into the foundations of existence. Only after the lessons from that wise man I told you about yesterday, did I slowly start to *understand* why I was striving like that, in that way. On the outside, my striving looks like sternness, and I really can't understand why everyone is so casual, so absolutely lazy in thinking, so driven by wishes and so completely not by the power of truth. Morality starts with pure, altruistic thinking, doesn't it? In it you come to the ideas of a free deed. Well, I've become like that, Maria. Still sunny and cheerful, but more on the inside, because I rejoice in gratitude. Because I was allowed to find the way, which a man *has* to find, if he truly wants to get to know happiness and sorrow.'

Maria was still trembling. The meeting with this man was like a landslide, or even stronger… the whole cosmos was shaking. Oh, she would not allow herself to fall in love. It was not about that at all. The love for him which she had felt at that time had been a recognition. She looked at him sideways as she spoke:

174

'At that time I already had the same questions as I have now, but elementary, not developed yet. I got stuck in them.... How will I ever find the relation between my scholarship, my knowledge of the human body and the reality of it? What I know is founded on experiential science. But that living, warm, pulsing, breathing body that a *human being* carries inside with thoughts and feelings, with conscience, that has remained a mystery. That is why I'm sitting at a desk as a school-doctor and not as a general practitioner or internist... then I truly wanted to have *knowledge* of my body, of the human body as a whole. Be in touch with it, live with it, suffer with it. You didn't give up, you carried on and, as you said, found the way. I'm still languishing, but I've become resigned... more or less. And then those touches of light that make me feel unwell... they urge me to seek further. I talk about it with Jean, but he has nothing else to say than: 'Read books on spirituality!'

'You could do that....' said Johannes with a smile.

'What would you advise?'

He remained silent for a while as he looked into the distance again.

She felt how *strong* his mind was. How can you feel something like that? She felt it... and shivered. He said:

'You could search for it in the work of the 'Master of the West'. You'd find your way. But I'd rather see you thinking through the sentences that I gave you yesterday, meditating and holding them. You can take in cart-loads of wisdom, but you won't become wiser from it if it doesn't become a *power* within you.'

She said, ashamed:

'I haven't been able to hold on to them completely; it was rather turbulent at home.'

'Try them now?'

She blushed from shyness. He was a real professor, after all... she dug in her memory.

'What's your greatest talent? the wise man asked you. You said: my understanding. And to his question what your greatest obstacle was, you answered that it's your brains. That's a paradox, isn't it? Your talent is your obstacle at the same time?'

'Understanding is larger than brains... you'd have to research these things in meditation. With all the strength that you have. Now, you're doing very well. Go on.'

'The he asked: what's the greatest riddle and you answered – I would've said the same: that man has to die. What is dying? Is there a life before birth, after death? Why do we know nothing about that?

Then he asked you what hurts you the most and you actually answered the same as I would have: goodbyes.

And then the task....'

She had to think for a long time. It was as if she was casting about in nothingness, in a bottomless depth.... What did he have to do? Try to understand dying... no... 'You had to try to understand goodbyes and then you would conquer your brains, your obstacle, because you understand dying.'

'Very good.'

'It doesn't tell me a lot, Johannes. At least... it makes me shiver.'

'Meditate on shivering... and you'll see that from these

176

few sentences the greatness of existence will blossom. First from thinking, feeling and willing – and finally also from the body. You'll have to be able to accept these touches of light and not become unstable because of them. Find the *power*, Maria!'

'What did he say?' Jean asked immediately when she came home.

She smiled at him and said with twinkling eyes:

'May I come in first?'

'Did you make another appointment with him?'

'Jean! Come on… he is going back to Amsterdam this afternoon.'

Everywhere on the farm there were people, children.… She walked upstairs, to the bedroom and flopped down on the couch. Jean sat next to her, put his arm around her shoulders and said:

'I'm trying not to be jealous, Maria… and I'm not afraid anymore. I'm only curious, because we both know that you're at a crossroads. Your questions will find their answers, but the journey will be long – will there still be a place for a simple chap like me?'

'So still afraid.…' she mumbled. She put her hand on his knee and said: 'He's given me a couple of sentences to meditate on. No answers, but a method, a *path*. Perhaps the answers lie along that path, but the journey will be long and I'm happy to take you with me, Jean. You don't have to let me go alone. I'd like to share everything with you. Johannes is a teacher, not a friend. Even though a modern spiritual teacher is more like a friend than he used to be in the past, I believe.'

After she had told him accurately what she had heard, Jean said:

'Steiner.'

'Why?' she asked, astonished.

'He's a follower of Steiner. I recognize the method. The Master of the West; it's him. I read about it in the past, but rather forgot it.'

'He's really *not* an anthroposopher, Jean!'

'He's too independent, too great… to be a member of a club. Still, every word that you received from him is a testimony of Steiner.'

'The Master of the West?'

'The West doesn't know of any Masters… except Steiner, and perhaps… Johannes.'

Her father had died. Her greatest teacher had withdrawn into an invisible, inaudible, elusive area… there where Being and Nothingness 'coexist'. The real, great farewell is death. You can imagine that the other is still there, you can even perceive it. But you cannot find the other anymore as completely and *definitely* present as they are during life on earth. You have your memories, part of your development is thanks to the other… but he will never be sitting there anymore, beneath that apple tree or at the kitchen table. His blue eyes will never look at you so intensely and you will never hear his contemplations anymore. They might still be there, his answers, perhaps more vividly and truly than ever, but your ears won't hear them….

178

What is the relationship between life in a body and this farewell through death? Where does all the seeing, hearing, and feeling completely end? She had always thought that all inner content originated from the senses. Careful inner investigation always brought her come back to that thought with certainty. But Johannes had pointed her to something else, to death itself, that could not possibly come from the senses, from the impressions. Not the content, but the *form* of the thoughts is sense-free. Indeed there is no *life* in them, you are in the shadow of death... but the form is sense-free; it is the spirit itself that casts its shadow there. She had worried and yearned too long for something essential in life to understand directly what Johannes had given her. But a concept was something relative here too. A concept is the first step, but in itself it is something lifeless, as all thinking is. The mind is the obstacle... one comes to feel at a distance from the whole of existence. The mind is at the same time the greatest gift; it liberates one and makes one confident. She had to investigate herself; what needs to be grasped in order to move from mere concept to *power* of thought?

*

Agnes received the message that her father was dying when she was at work in the ward. The stroke came completely unexpectedly. Of course he was old now and eventually the moment of farewell would come, but not yet – not for a long time. Then so suddenly, there it was; fate struck like a dagger through her anxious heart. She left immediately in her fast car, heading south. René would come later, with or without their four young children.

A hospital, normally her trusted place of work, suddenly seemed a dangerous place. There, in intensive care, lay her father, no longer responsive. A fragile, little man of the country, one of the many patients… some got better, some didn't. This little farmer would die within several hours. An ordinary little man. On the inside she was screaming! He was the most special, wise, sweet man alive! *Her* father! Not just a fruit farmer at the end of his, perhaps, pious life – a sweetheart, so full of understanding of what was incomprehensible to her!

Maria was serenity itself, as always. She sat next to mom at his bed; she had prepared for this moment, wise as she was. To her, death was not an end, but a transition. Maria was so wise, you could almost believe her…. Agnes could not feel it that way. Gone is gone! This body would become still, motionless. It would be put in the ground and that would be that for daddy…. The thought was unbearable; that was the reason why people had invented the notion of life after death, so this terrible thing would not have to be experience. She stood at the other side of the bed. Two daughters, two doctors. Yet they did not know what to do to keep him here. She took his small, warm hand in hers. She had not known that she loved him this much… she too had expected so much still! He had to tell her what life is about. Not about money, sex, glory. What then? Waves of despair almost overwhelmed her. Tears, warm and

180

salty, started to stream down her cheeks and flow into her mouth. 'Come on, Agnes!' Maria berated.

She shook her head desperately.

'I can't help it!' she sobbed. 'He can't die, I love him so much. He's always so sweet.... I've let everything go by, everything!'

Maria took her to the hallway and said calmly:

'Think about mom. This is the worst for her. We have our own life.'

'You don't understand,' Agnes sobbed out loud. 'You don't understand at all! You took your chances to be with him; I didn't. He must stay for a while, Maria!'

Maria hugged her and caressed her hair.

'It's all right, we'll get through this. Come on, we're going to go back now. Control yourself, Agnes!'

He died without saying goodbye to them. Agnes, the skilled surgeon, ran out of the room in shock. She could not look at her father's lifeless body. René, who had arrived in the meantime, tried to comfort her. But there was no comfort here... when you died yourself one day, you would feel the same. A whole life wasted on meaningless things and now eye to eye with the eternal Judge: 'You merely enjoyed your talents!' The judgment would be very strict and you would feel that you had failed to do *everything* that you should have done. This was a foretaste; it just applied to the relationship with *one* man, her father. But then *every* relationship would be judged. What was she thinking, fantasising? Still it seemed to be true, for she felt it. This was moral panic, complete chaotic panic. She drummed on

René's chest with her fists.

'You don't get it! Nobody gets it! He was a miracle, and I didn't believe it! Now, in his absence, I *know*! A miracle, René!'

'I do know that, love. I also knew him, didn't I?'

Agnes wailed like an actor in a Greek tragedy. Wailing and moaning, crying and gnashing of teeth. Nobody could comfort her.

She cried continuously until she fell asleep, exhausted. The next morning she woke up bathed in sweat. Jet cared for the children; she herself was not able to do anything. René tried to talk to her, to bring her to reason, but she simply did not *want* reasonableness. Death overthrows all reasonableness; there is no concept at all with which you can confront it. Before it lies beauty, wisdom and power – after it, only the great nothingness, the *non*sense, the denial of all your zest for life. Death comes for everyone, without exception. Even God Incarnate had to give way to him, although they said: only for three days. As a child she had learned that he had conquered death. As a grown-up you could not believe that anymore. Although... death was irrationality itself, a negative miracle, something incomprehensible. Why should it not be possible that it could be overcome with something as incomprehensible? Why should life remain subject to death until eternity? And the relation would never, never turn around? Miracles do not occur in the twentieth century anymore... except for the miracle with a minus: Death.

Her mother came to her regularly, took her to her bosom like a child and shook her head in silence. She did not cry; she had daddy with her, secure in her heart. To her, nothingness was everything and the nowhere was everywhere. Then, at the heart of her mother, she felt quiet for a while. The comfort was like what she had felt when she was a child when she was in pain or when she was sad. They had had a blessed childhood with such parents in such an environment. When she thought about how she had raised her own children... every day to the crèche, in the evening she was tired and impatient, it was all too much for her. The children hung on her, that was cute, but they whined, cried, fought. She gave them a vicious smack now and then, which made the misery even worse. Finally, René came out of his study and gave a lecture on how neurosis and psychasthenia originates. Oedipus appeared on the scene, and Agnes got violently sick. Then René and she started to fight and the chaos was complete. *Four* children, why not just one or two? Sometimes it was cosy too... the children also used to adore grandfather, who could tell such beautiful stories and listened so attentively to their gossip. In the summer all four could stay on the farm, so Agnes and René were able to go on a holiday together for two weeks. They got their children back as docile lambs, completely soaked with attention and love. For the children it was also a disaster that grandfather was dead. Dead... stone-dead. Then the sobbing began again, desperately, incontinently, without an end....

Maria sat with her father's body; Agnes did not understand how she could do it. She had tried it too, but already fled after half a minute. The spiritless body instilled horror in her. She had been confronted with death so many times and she had never realized how *bad* dying actually is. Perhaps not to the dying person, but to the ones staying behind... my God! Why were they all so quiet and resigned!? And she so completely desperate? Because she was the worst of everyone? Because she was afraid of the weighing of her soul? Hell? Oh, she feared the Nothingness like everybody else. Only her solution was more sincere: *none*!

But why did the Holy Mass get to her so much? The coffin in the middle aisle, the church completely packed.... everyone knew her father.... the organ raged through her soul, the choir tormented her ears.... she would go crazy, the famous psychiatrist's wife had become psychotic... the burden had become too heavy for her weak little person. Was her state a case of decompensation? No, no! Agnes was *strong*! She burst into tears again, her body trembled because of the suppressed grief. Daddy! Hail, thou true body! *Ave verum corpus.* Dreadful music, but so painfully beautiful now....

René was worried; he did not allow her to go to the grave. She did not want to; she was exhausted. This would pass, he felt. She gave in to his protection, perhaps for the first time. She heard his words, but did not understand them. She only heard the sound of his voice; it made her feel safe. The lightning could not strike her; he built a fortress around her.

184

'Johannes is here too. Did you see him?' René asked.

She rebounded.

'How sweet of him to come. I want to talk to him!'

René drove to the restaurant where a lunch was to be held. He said:

'I asked him to come to the lunch. He would come for a moment. For you.'

She sighed deeply. He would know how to comfort her, even though his way of thinking was not hers. They had remained friends. It had been a painful blow for her when he had finally found the love of his life. She, Agnes, had not been the one for him and she was curious as to what kind of woman he had chosen. It turned out that it was not a woman, but a girl, a student, an innocent child.... She had realised when she saw her. Johannes' choice was a synthesis of Agnes and Maria, the pure middle between the two: innocence without fear, courage with modesty, beauty without narcissism. Agnes was present at the marriage and had *truly* seen what kind of man Johannes was. He was actually a *human being* more than he was a man. His wife would understand how to use the freedom that he granted her and would commit herself to his whole being. Agnes would *never* have been able to do that; married to Johannes, she would not have reached the point of being able to see who he truly was. She could only see that from a distance, as a spectator in the audience. She would see him later; he had remained connected to her life as she had with his. After all, she had to thank him for saving her relationship with René... and so much more!

When the invitees eventually arrived, she withdrew to a corner of the room. How was it possible that these people were talking and laughing with each other as if it was a wedding! She loathed it and looked at her plate disapprovingly, without eating or drinking anything. Now and then somebody approached her, but she did not engage in conversation; they could all drop dead as far as she was concerned! Where was Johannes?

At last he arrived....

'I first took Eva home, she was tired... she is expecting.'

For him, she got up from her chair. She stood in front of him, full of expectation. He looked at her for a long time and took her by the shoulders firmly.

'I've noticed how difficult it is for you, Agnes,' he said softly. 'I'm so sorry for you. You loved him a lot.'

She bowed her head and said:

'If only I had known *how* much! Why do we realise this only now, when it's too late?'

'It's not too late... the fact that you feel now how much you loved him shows how *good* he was, doesn't it? It's your powerlessness, Agnes, that you're feeling. That hurts, I know that, but the pain's not without a reason, believe me.'

'I wish I could believe you. I do believe you – and yet I don't. You must meet my sister... there she is.'

'She's busy with all the family and acquaintances. Let her be... I'll meet her later. But you, Agnes! Will you be *strong*, like you are?'

She shook her head:

'Strong... in narcissism, yes. But now, eye to eye with the

186

end, I'm *nothing*, Johannes.'

'In nothingness lives pure being.'

'I'm afraid that my nothingness is really *nothing*. I can do two things: get into a depression or become hard, even harder than I already was. Just forget about everything and go on with partying.'

He looked at her seriously. She longed for physical comfort, an arm around her shoulder. She had to be satisfied with a hand on her shoulder and an embrace with his look. He said, a little sternly:

'They're both *weak*, Agnes. Feel what you're feeling! There's no other cure than enduring your feelings… then you'll get through this. It's a catharsis; you'll be purified by it and will be stronger than before.'

'Perhaps I hate purification,' she sulked.

Johannes burst into a laugh.

'Yes, yes. I'm going now. I'll be staying with my parents for a few more days. You can always call me.'

He kissed her on the cheek, turned around and walked away, tall and straight. Righteous.

He met her sister twice at the graveyard. Agnes was wildly angry about it. It had always been that way. Maria stole all her friends. She knew exactly how to do that, with her hypocrisy. Agnes never had a friendship for herself, she had even had to share René with her sister all these years! She paid Maria back by ignoring her completely. After two days, Maria asked:

'What's wrong, Agnes?! What have I done to you? You're not the only one who's grieving. It doesn't justify how you're behaving.'

'Mind your own business, will you? There's a lot wrong with your behaviour too.'

'Tell me, so I can do something about it.'

'You're stealing my friends again.'

Maria looked at her fiercely:

'What're you talking about?!'

'About your rendezvous with Johannes.'

'You wanted us to meet, didn't you?'

'Not like that. So idyllically at the grave.'

Maria laughed at her.

'He wanted it that way; he didn't want to come over here.'

Agnes was furious.

'What is so special about Maria!' she cried.

'Nothing. What does the meeting with Johannes have to do with you and me? I could also say: Agnes took René from me.'

'You were only too happy about that. You are and will remain a bitch.'

Maria became calm. She sighed.

'Let it be. I've talked to him twice and that was it. He remains *your* friend. Don't worry.'

'What were you talking about?'

'About death. The best theme at a graveside.'

She was reassured. Maria was an interesting type, with a trashy job and a 'salon husband'. Only when you were in trouble could she be of any use.

Grief and anger alternated in Agnes. She fell asleep crying and woke up furious, or lay awake angry and awoke from a short sleep in tears.... René did his utmost to understand her, but she only poured out her powerlessness on him. She hated his understanding as much as his attempts to comfort her…. According to him, she was a hysteria; he had his diagnosis ready. She tyrannised the whole family: Jean held his breath continuously when he witnessed her constant, challenging nagging; her mother did her best to comfort her. Maria tried to bring her to reason with words and René felt responsible.

Agnes enjoyed her power…. What did she want? In any case she did *not* want to feel the powerlessness she *was* feeling. She completely forgot that it was about daddy. She forgot that he was dead… he could walk into the room any moment.

'We must be going home, Agnes,' René said at night. 'It's about time we got back to our own lives.'

She started crying. Own lives? She *had* no life. He tried to comfort her, but she pushed him away. She wanted him to comfort her… ah, that constantly returning despair. Like when one approaches suicide. End it immediately, so you won't have to wait patiently until the moment comes. Crying was weakness, and she hated weakness. But the despair was stronger than her power.

'What's wrong, my love?' René asked softly, in another attempt to understand her. 'Daddy was not that important to you, was he?'

'He *was*, but I didn't know. *That* is wrong, René, a missed opportunity without hope for a second chance.'

'Every relationship is an opportunity, also the one between me and you.'

'You're an ordinary guy. My father was a miracle.'

189

'You always repeat the same thing. What good does it do? You must move on, Agnes.'

She had to move on… they went back to The Hague, she resumed her work, locked up her grief deep inside her feelings. She was the strong Agnes again, full of life. Pretty, ambitious and vital. She wore armour around her heart, so it would never, never again be struck like it was when daddy died….

When, a couple of years later, her mother also died, she did not shed a tear. Not because she had loved her less, but because she had in the meantime armoured her heart. She saw the strike coming and warded it off before she got hit. She 'used her brains', which helped her to remain reasonable and helped with the settlement of all the affairs. The farm had to be sold, the possessions divided, the inheritance paid out …. Everything passed off harmoniously with her sister, who was always calm throughout. Maria had trouble saying goodbye to the parental home with the courtyard and the apple trees… but she had already said goodbye years ago – when daddy died.

'...any exhibiting of an entity as it shows itself in itself may be called 'phenomenology' with formal justification.'

Martin Heidegger (1889 - 1976)

It was a long walk to the place where Maria had parked her car. She had not seen a lot of the environment anymore because of all the memories that she had along the way. Ten years had gone by since her father's death – and the meeting with Johannes. Ten years of intensive study and meditation. She had followed her path independently. She was able to, and had had to do it that way. She had read Johannes' books but had never met him again. Her meeting with him at her father's grave had been an absolute turning point in her life, although there was nothing to notice on the outside. She still had the same job, the same house... the same husband. The children had left home; they were now studying at university. Her youth had passed, and normally one came into a closing phase after one's fifties. But she had the feeling that her life had only truly started ten years ago. Before that, there had been an unsatisfied longing, in which everything was steeped. She lived on old forces that seemed to be a gift, forces that gradually ran down... just at their nadir the new had presented itself to her. At first, it had only been words, spoken by a man, by Johannes. Those words had gained meaning and *power* by meditating on them. They had become effects that had changed her, that fulfilled her, very slowly but with complete certainty, with answers, with gratification of that indeterminate longing. The melancholy had not diminished; on the contrary… but she was not indeterminate anymore. Her melancholy had become a living effect; all her thoughts and feelings became living effects. Sometimes she could long painfully for another conversation with that man who was now distant, about whom she heard something from Agnes now and then. He had increasingly got into difficulties with his position at the hospital, conscientious objections with regard to what he had to stand for – and had ultimately withdrawn from his profession in order to devote himself completely to that other task, to the development of *spiritual* science.

In Jean she had a friend with whom she did everything together, including the study of that spiritual science. There was only *one* point on which she could not find agreement with him… that was her relationship with Johannes. He did not want that, absolutely not. He also read Johannes' books, without any criticism. But his person was a threat. Maria adapted to Jean's feelings. She did not see a possibility of turning to Johannes without completely disturbing of the harmony between herself and Jean – so she did not. Still, it was a kind of denial, which tormented her. If she talked to Jean about it, they would start arguing. They would make up again, but there was no solution. Was it personal jealousy… or something else?

Agnes also obviously had an interest in the fact that Maria and Johannes did not meet again. She always spoke about him with pride, but always with some clear indication that he was *her* friend. Perhaps Maria was too docile, perhaps she should break right across all the resistance. But she did not.... When she was reading Steiner, she thought: *he* should *be* here now, in this terrible, difficult time, to show the way to those people who seek the spirit – not only through his works, which are already available, but through his personal presence. Well, she did not think that Johannes and Steiner were the same individuality – she experienced a different essence in Johannes, but she could not be certain in that area. Should she not do *everything* that was in her power to make the most of his presence on earth? Ten years of inner work in loneliness. Didn't her whole being yearn for the elaboration of her spiritual relationship with Johannes?

For what does one actually live? For love and freedom. Both are given to you in a certain way, but you have to work yourself to double those two human qualities *here and now*, triple them... enlarge them infinitely. One has one's faith... one's profession, talents, husband and children. In accepting these, the surrender to faith, lives your love. You live with your faith through the degree of love assigned to you ... you cannot go above it, or beneath it. That can only be done with freedom.

Freedom can be searched for, in and through consciousness. Freedom exists, as far as one is free from *everything* that can bind one. Free from God as well as from your fellow men, religion and upbringing. There where nothing else rules you than you yourself, you can choose - the good or the bad. You can use your freedom for yourself in an absolute egoism. You can also bind your free impulses with love…. Her faith bound her to Jean, her freedom to Johannes. How should those two be connected in the right way?

She had been sitting beneath the apple tree too long, now she had to walk the whole way back to the car. Jean always thought it was worrisome when she went for a walk alone, but she knew the hills and the paths so well. Jean was a special man; he lived with her in complete equality. She saw that nowhere else, not with any other couple. A woman could be so independent and have a big mouth, but the last word was invariably still with the man. Superficial observation could not always see that, but a slightly deeper view of reality brought that old, supposedly superseded hierarchy into the light. Only Jean consciously did not do that. His appreciation for her being was such that it did not matter which of them 'wore the trousers'. Therefore, she gave in to his reluctance concerning her friendship with Johannes. It was no ambition for power, but powerlessness. He was not afraid of anything…. When she looked back on her life, she saw a wonderful combination of happiness and melancholy. Outwardly everything had gone on smoothly, but that blessing was always accompanied by an internal longing…. The essence of existence had eluded her – until she met Johannes. At first that meeting had filled a void… later that void had become stronger, more tangible. Those light touches, which always made her stagger, had transferred more to the inside; they came from the inside and, enlightening the void, strengthened the feeling of powerlessness.

194

But they were accompanied by an increasing disclosure of *power*, because of which her feeling of powerlessness was caught and transformed. She thought it was a sort of martyrdom, only flushed with feelings of mercy. Everything was deprivation, and just that deprivation turned out to be mercy....

In the distance she saw a stranger approaching; he or she was walking in the opposite direction. Sometimes a bend in the road hid the figure from the eye, and then the next moment she saw it again, a little closer. One could happen on an unfortunate incident in this way... well, she was no longer a little girl, but one should actually have a dog if one wanted to take such walks. Turning back made no sense; she would not get home at all. Ah, something like this only happens when God wants it to happen – and then it should.... It was a small man, of indeterminate age. Not a frightening type at all. She felt a silent calm in her melancholic feeling. Everything is actually all right, however it may go. She apparently had the task in her life to experience the enormous discrepancy between body and spirit. The imprisonment in the body and the unbelievable longing for liberation – without truly dying. Everybody in the end is liberated at the moment of death. But she longed for a similar liberation during life. She had worked at it and worked hard. She had spent a large part of her spare time on filling her thoughts with spirit, on raising tem beyond ordinary thinking and feeling. Little by little she had gained power and achieved valuable moments of freedom. But she had the feeling that she was capable of *more*. Everything in life wants to tie man to his body. That *every-thing* has to be achieved without complaining about the barriers - she felt that so strongly now.... at the approach of that small figure... that everything is *good*, as long as you are striving intensely. Surrender to what fate brings you... even the apparently bad years are good, because you need them. You want to develop yourself and that can only be done with resistance. Nobody thinks that it is strange that one develops physical strength with the aid of resistance. In an era where fitness training has become a popular form of leisure activity, everyone should know that power arises from going against resistance... why would that be different in the inner life?

She was able to see him well now. He had an extraordinary flexible walk, although he was older than she was, perhaps not.... He really looked at her... he was not sunk in thought, but he saw her. It comforted her to be seen by him, one was actually not often really *seen*. He was really walking there for *her*... coming towards her. She shivered. You could run into someone just like that... someone who wants to kill you or someone to share your life with... a master, an initiate... a simple walker who has put himself on your path. Even the Lord Himself can show Himself to you in mercy if He wants to. You could meet Him just like that, or He could enter your room, just at the moment of your greatest need. *'One who sits alone in his room, weeping heavy, bitter tears....* Of course nobody believes that, in a time when miracles are no longer accepted. Miracles are for childish people, for primitives. We, on the other hand, have made such wonderful progress with science that we no longer have to be afraid of the unexplainable. For everything is explainable; miracles do not exist.

She saw miracles every day.... newborns, infants, toddlers, preschoolers, primary school children - one miracle after another. The whole macrocosm had contracted into a human body, went through death and of course, as the power of the macrocosm, resurrected. Since then that macrocosmic power has lived – invisible to the senses – together with the earth and exposes itself in the transcendent to whomsoever He wants, when He wants. The kingdom of Shamballa must be searched for on earth, but not in the physical atmosphere perceptible to the senses... the approaching walker caused her to think these thoughts.

'Christ once lived on Earth.... She knew these ideas about the advent of Christ in the etheric world from the work of Rudolf Steiner... but this man seemed to be of flesh and blood. He was still several metres away from her and he was still looking at her. She stood still... he came towards her. God knows how such a thing is possible, here on this path through the fields – that a well-prepared meeting occurs. Without an appointment, but definitely no coincidence.
'May I walk with you for a little?' the stranger asked. 'I have something to tell you.'
She nodded. All physical heaviness was gone, she only felt youthfulness, a life that was tender but highly defined.... A life that sounded like a symphony, in strange tones on unknown instruments, sounding in colour... dying had to

be such a blessing, the transition to a purely spiritual existence, the triumph of the spirit. But she was not dying; she was walking along a small path through the fields... next to her an angel on her path... a messenger... or...?

'You have just let your life pass before your spiritual eyes in memories. Memory bans you into physical existence. Now I will raise you to a pure spiritual observation of your present life, so that you will in time become aware of its truth and meaning.'

He was silent for a long time, as Maria cherished his words in her mind. Then his voice sounded again:

'But the Spirit does not speak for your sake. Everything that you hear is self-knowledge, but is meant for the good development of all mankind. You therefore need to unite with the man who is waiting for you. Demons will fight you, but do not fear. Be led by your sincere longing. Its purity is your guide.'

She bore her heart in humility, her head as high as the starry sky. Above her, she saw the rising moon.... And when she looked next to her again, he was gone. Had he ever been there? Oh yes, she could have touched him! Did he go onto a side-path? She had not seen a side-path. The world was filled with spirit... she saw her life path to the future very clear now – as her past showed itself to her in perfection.

Jean was outside on the street waiting for her.

'Why didn't you at least have your phone on!' he said angrily. 'I've been worried sick!'

She hugged him and said:

'The battery was dead. You're right, I haven't paid attention to the time.'

They walked inside; the table was set.

'You know how much I disapprove of your solitary hikes!' he grumbled on. 'Who knows who you could run into?'

'Chance doesn't exist,' she said resolutely. 'Later, after dinner, I will tell you about what I experienced. Now I feel like that delicious salad that you have made.'

Was she allowed to talk about the meeting? She could not live on alongside Jean and not tell him about the greatest happening in her life. She was free to decide what she wanted to do.

She did not tell him yet; it was too soon. She had to let the experience sink in, let it grow. Then she would discuss it with him. Tomorrow... or the day after tomorrow.

Her memories were transformed into impulses, egoistic and altruistic. She did not see the ordinary, pale memory images, but lived in the occurrences as if they were present, only without remembering the physical reality in images. She experienced the urge of faith in her motives and sometimes the gloss of freedom.... A moral impulse streamed like a beautiful river through the withered land of egoistic drifting sands....

'Jean... it's difficult for me to tell you this... but I have to make contact with Johannes.'

He pulled an ugly face. She hated that face, because an ugly feature was expressed by it. But one does not see oneself… who knows how ugly one looks sometimes.

Before he could say something, she started to tell him about her meeting on that Thursday afternoon, just before the evening….

'Why are you telling me this now? It's Sunday already!' he asked indignantly.

'Is that your only reaction?' she asked sternly.

'Sorry, it's jealousy. *I* am a simple guy; *you* experience miracles.'

'Nonsense. If I share them with you, you experience them too. At least if you're not locking yourself up in your jealousy.'

'I want to go with you to meet Johannes.'

'It didn't occur to me to go without you.'

'OK, call him up. We'll take a two-week holiday and travel to Switzerland - where he is now.'

She could not believe it. For ten years she had waited to ask him this… and it was accepted in five minutes.

'I expected you'd put up huge resistance,' she said. 'Do I know you that badly? What kind of relationship *is* this?'

He took his head in his hands and sighed very deeply.

'I'm sorry, Maria. You do know me very well. Without the story about that man during the walk I would've put up some strong resistance. If I did that now too… I'd be making a big mistake. I have a big problem with that Johannes.'

'You've never really *seen* him before!'

'I have a big problem with him… I don't know. It *is* jealousy. Of him, of you, the two of you… of what'll happen between you two.'

She needed a couple of days, before she had the courage to call the spiritual institute where Johannes had been working for a couple of years now. She did not want to ask Agnes for the number; she did not feel like nagging. She got a number from the telephone directory service. A German-speaking lady came on the phone.

'Can I talk to the professor?' she asked hesitantly. She thought it was a ridiculous question. She was put through to a secretary. She repeated her question.

'He is in a meeting right now. If you give me your phone number, I'll ask him to call you back.'

'When can I expect his call, then?'

'Between twelve and one this afternoon.'

She gave her number and hung up. Of course he would not call back; he could not start with that, could he? Nowadays it was always said: he or she is in a meeting, you will be called back – and you never heard of him or her again.

Between twelve and one anyone who could call called… and at 12.45, when she had almost forgotten that she was waiting for a call, she heard:

'This is Leven, I've been given this number to call back.'

She had to swallow. It was not strange that Jean was jealous. She felt a very strong connection to this man. She said:

'Johannes, this is Maria, Agnes' sister…'

The voice at the other end remained silent.

'Remember… we spoke at the grave of my father.'

'Of course I remember.'

Did she hear emotion in his voice? Ah… she was not that important. In any case, she felt strong emotion herself, *so* strong that she went on with difficulty:

'I… uh… would like to meet you again. I don't know how you work… how it's organized there, but… could I come and visit some day?'

Again, he remained silent. If she could only see him… on the phone one has no idea of the expression of the one on the other end of the line. At last, he said:

'In the summer it's very busy here, I wouldn't be able to welcome you in the right way. You could come now, very soon, or in September. You're very welcome, Maria.'

It was definitely emotion that she heard in his voice. She said:

'I want to come as soon as possible. I've waited too long already. Jean will be coming with me.'

'Of course. Name the date.'

She arranged a date; he would take care of the accommodation. She had seen him only twice, except for those months during her studies when he had been a practicals assistant. Today she spoke to him for the third time and she had the feeling of coming home after a long, long journey full of deprivation.

*

Agnes had developed her strength fighting against the wind. She had seen her life go by while she walked against the wind along the coast. Gradually, she had developed an unpleasant feeling, which she had more and more often lately in all kinds of circumstances. It seemed like labour contractions, only the cramps were not in her belly, but in her

202

chest. She got a lame jaw because of it… she was no general practitioner or internist but she had diagnosed it immediately: angina pectoris. Fear, hate, doubt and stress… had planted germs of disease inside her coronary artery system, it cramped or it was closed…. It was very bad right now… and she had to walk back for kilometres, indeed with the wind at her back. She turned around. What a relief. She searched in her pockets for the strip of tablets for under her tongue, and took one. It did not really help. Perhaps she would get a heart attack here on the beach. A fifty year-old woman, in the prime of life. She had to do something about it. René… she would not tell him. He would say: tomorrow you will go to friend my so and so, a cardiologist. He would take it all very seriously and within one or two weeks she would have surgery. No… she would go to Johannes; he would know what to do. With him you had the feeling that you were a *human being*, unique and thus irreplaceable. Not a number with a statistic survival chance of so many percent. She was a convinced materialist, someone who had put everything on one card: the body. Her father's death had made her falter. She knew that Johannes had a different view of medicine… but her respect for him was so great that she did not mock him for it. Now there was something wrong with her, she even saw only *one* real doctor in the large circle of colleagues around her….

'Johannes, I need your advice, medical advice. When can I visit you?'

'I'm not next door, Agnes. What's wrong?'

'Heart disease. Severe, believe me.'

'I can recommend a good cardiologist, a friend.'

'I don't need a cardiologist. I want you.'

It was silent for a while. Then he said:

'All right. Come immediately. Tomorrow or the day after tomorrow, I have time now.'

'I'll look for a flight on the Internet and call you back.'

She hung up, satisfied. She still loved that noble man in the mountains very much. This was a perfect occasion to see him again.

At the airport she rented a car and drove to the clinic in the mountains, where Johannes worked nowadays. On the way she thought about René, who was at home alone with four children of whom three were deep into the strains of puberty. In the end, she had told him why she wanted to go to Johannes; she needed René's cooperation. He was a sweetheart... he was frightened to death and had called her in sick immediately and took a week off himself. Doctors have little empathy, so she did not want to have surgery. She knew too well how that went... well, of course it could be releasing, such surgery. First let's wait to see what Johannes has to say.

She drove through the little streets of a mountain village, followed the twisting road upward, to the valley situated even further up: beautiful, those high rising mountains, the peaks covered with snow. The clinic was part of a large residential centre; she would get a room in the main building. It was impressively situated in a big park, perfectly maintained... everything about Johannes was impressive....

She was disappointed that he was not there to welcome her. The receptionist knew that she was coming, she got a key and a note with a time and a place of her appointment with the great man here.... The room also disappointed her. It was on the second floor, while there were also rooms on the first floor with folding-doors to a private terrace. She had to be satisfied with a balcony and a dazzling view on the mountains. She had expected to be welcomed as the great friend, but she was just one of the many. Well, she could always go home again and go to René's friend, the cardiologist.

He did not welcome her in his medical office in the clinic, but in a room in the main building. She did not see an examination couch, she saw a desk with chairs and three walls with books. He wore his usual blue blazer and looked perfect like always. His face was serious, and she had the unpleasant feeling that he did not like the fact that she was here.

She received a firm handshake and was asked to sit down.

'I was startled by your complaints,' he said, nevertheless friendly and warm.

He was like the sun that enlightens and warms. The only loyal friend a man has. You know that he will always be there. She felt like crying on his chest... but she said:

'It might disturb you that I come here just like this, but I didn't know what else to do. I really need your judgment, your advice, your wise advice.'

'Have you ever followed it, my 'wise advice'?'

Astonished, she answered:

'That sounds bitter. Why?'

He shook his head. 'It's a common bitterness. In this time of self-consciousness, people do want advice, but they only want to hear what they would advise themselves. It's an exhausting occupation, Agnes, when one has to give advice like that.'

She thought about it and said:

'That's true, yes. Mostly what you say is not what I want to hear – so I follow my own ideas. That's freedom.'

'Then leave me alone, will you?'

'What's the matter with you?! You used to be so open, so cordial, so benevolent!'

He smiled.

'I'm testing your motivation for coming here.'

'And? What's the result?' she asked irritably.

'Of course, I'll do what you ask me,' he said calmly. 'I'll examine you, have them do a supplementary examination and give you the diagnosis that you already have. Subsequently, I'll give you advice, advice about how to handle it, and my judgment as to how you got it. The rest is up to you. That's your freedom.'

She really felt like crying now. She bowed her head and said softly:

'Come on, Johannes. I have great faith in you, I need you. Where are you…?'

'This is more than a clinic here. First, this was a school for Eastern wisdom, a meditation centre. The master from the East is still here…. He was very strict; if one wanted to come here for a course, one had to be ready to live like

206

a monk for several weeks. One had to subject oneself to a strict regime. We, the master and myself, work here together. His policy is contradictory to western freedom; we have dispensed with it, transformed it. The consequence is that we have a lot of tourists here who look for a bit of spirituality without seriousness, without that complete devotion that is needed. You're not here for spirituality, but for your health. Of course I can help you, but my diligence works in the spirit, in the soul – not directly in the body. If you want my help, *after* I've done what you've asked me to do, you'll have to surrender your freedom to a certain discipline – and it'll be hard for you, because I know you, Agnes. You've developed; so have I. I'm no longer that cheerful friend that I used to be, nor that strict, very capable professor.'

'Who are you now then, Johannes?' she asked desperately. She looked up, into his big blue eyes.

'I am Johannes,' he said, smiling. 'I searched for the spirit, and I found it. It's as big as the cosmos and even bigger; as extensive as eternity and more. I investigate the spirit, and engage in spiritual science. As your friend, I'll do what you ask of me. Will you as my friend take seriously what my deepest striving is?'

Suddenly she understood what he meant, what he was asking. He was asking for honesty. She could not come here and ask while not respecting his way of answering; that was insincere. She could not mock the spirit – like she always did – and still want to have the fruits of it. She bowed her head again, this time really in shame and said:

'All right, Johannes, I have understood what you mean.

I'll first consider if I can be your friend in that way, and get your advice. May I come back tomorrow?'

He nodded and got up.

'Come at the same time, Agnes. I'll look forward to your arrival.'

Overwhelmed, she walked outside. She felt like a little girl in search for love... and rejected. She sat on a bench. Here and there some people were walking, in little groups. They were here for spirituality, or perhaps also for physical healing. She felt a deep, disconsolate loneliness. It was not fair. All good impulses in her life arose from her friendship with Johannes; was that not enough? His integrity had made her feel how insincere she was, then... she had straightened things out with René because of it. And there were more things like that.... Now she had the feeling that she was losing his friendship, and it hurt her unbearably. She got up with a stretch. Once she had determined to ignore sorrow and point her attention to something else. She had also ignored that sickly pain in her chest as much as possible. Sometimes the pain got so strong that she could not ignore it any more.... She walked off the path. In the distance on the right there was a house, a chalet. Did he live there? It was a gorgeous situation, completely free, with a terrace facing the majesty of the mountains. A man came out, an Indian man; he was probably in his late sixties, but looked very vital. That had to be 'the master'. She hoped that he would not come her way; she did not feel like a meeting with him. But sure enough, he saw her and came towards her. She felt she was just a passer-by; they would greet each other and walk on. She would look in front of

208

her and avoid his glance, and get past him. But just when he passed her she looked up and caught his glance. What dark eyes, what a depth…! She was startled by it. He stopped and said:

'You should not go into the mountains, madam. Heavy weather is coming.

She stopped herself and mumbled:

'I was just walking. I was going to turn around.'

'I am just telling you, it is dangerous. By the way, I do not know you, have you just arrived?'

'Do you know everyone who's staying here?'

He smiled.

'It is an old rule: the master wants to see and speak to everybody who comes here.'

'Also the patients?'

'No. Sometimes. Are you a patient?'

She put out her hand and gave her name.

'I'm Agnes, a friend of Johannes. We've known each other since our student days, or a little later. I don't want to refer to myself as a 'patient', but I did come here in connection with health problems.'

'Would you come in for a while, Agnes? Then we can talk a little and you will have had the obligatory talk with the master.'

He grinned and looked at her inquisitively. She was scared of the master, of the abyss in his eyes. But she was also lonely and a great warmth emanated from him. She nodded and followed him into his house. He took her to a room with thick carpets on the floor. There were only two simple chairs. Nothing else.

'This is my meditation room, Agnes. Sit down.'

Her fear increased. What was he going to do to her? Except for those thick carpets on the floor, it was as sombre as in a cell. She sat on the hard chair with the straight back. He pulled his chair closer and sat opposite of her. Was he going to charm her or put a spell on her?

'What kind of meditation do you do?' she asked nervously.

He smiled in a friendly way. He was as innocent as her father!

He did not answer but said:

'Agnes, Agnes... you are so frightened. Why are you so frightened?'

'I... er... don't know you, so....'

Shaking his head, he said:

'That is not what I mean, child. You are full of fear, beautifully shaped indeed, but fatal nevertheless. Admit now that you are frightened!'

She felt how convulsive she was and tried to relax a little.

'I'm not scared at all, never.'

'Child, child... you are misleading yourself. Come now,... who is Agnes actually? Has she ever grown up? Or is she still captured by the childish laws of being bad and getting punished?'

He spoke in both Dutch and English. The way he said 'Child, child....'

'I'm not scared!' she repeated stubbornly.

'A heart attack is founded on fear, years of fear.'

'I haven't had a heart attack. How do you know that I have heart problems?'

'I could see that as soon as I saw you. You live on forces that are not yours; it is all a big show.'

She heard her father talking. He would have spoken like that – if she had ever come that far, she would really have had a good talk with him.

'Do you know my father?' she asked and she thought: I am beginning to lose my mind!'

'He is here. In this moment.'

Oh, now she was frightened. Frightened to death. Frightened of the invisible, the inexplicable, the irrational, the illogical. Still, she was irrational herself often, a first class hysteric – she knew that well enough. All show.... One could not get angry with this man; he was like God Himself. When reality spoke, you had no defence. Afraid, yes. She shivered. Oh that pain... that constant pain. If she were only able to cry...

'How do you know...?' she asked weakly.

'Where you are, he is too.'

She had to pick herself up and get back into the light of day, instead of being in this twilight state on this miserable hard chair opposite this weird man.

'I want to leave,' she said.

To her astonishment, he got up immediately and said:

'Of course. This was the obligatory talk with the master.'

She did not actually want to leave at all, but now she had to. She shook his hand and said uncertainly:

'Thank you, master.'

Thanks... for what? Outside the sun had gone; heavy thunder was threatening. She was not afraid of that. She was never afraid!

'I've been thinking long and deeply, Johannes. You apparently have no idea how much influence your moral *being* has on my way of living. From the first day on, I've loved you and when it became clear that you did not want me, I transformed my love into friendship. I could no longer commit adultery and settled things with René; we have four children and I've been trying very hard. Of course I love myself a lot, perhaps that's not allowed in your view of things... but if there is *one* person for whom I have the deepest respect... it's you. You were harsh yesterday... I wouldn't have come here at all if I didn't have complete trust in you, also in your faith. It's easier not to have such a faith, so I don't. But now, with this severe heart problem, everything looks different. I'm fifty years old and I'm going to have a heart attack sooner or later, or I'll have to have surgery. Yesterday, I told someone that I'm not afraid. But I am, I'm afraid of death, of the nothingness that might be the everything... and of the reprimand that I've believed in nothing. I *am* afraid, Johannes! That's why I came here, to you. Who else? Which doctor gives a damn about how I feel? Help me, Johannes!'

Two wonderful men, the master and Johannes. They both threw you in the deep end and watched what happened. Johannes was behind his desk, stern and unreachable. She had fallen into a fairy tale, with witchcraft and impossible tasks.... But he spoke to her in a friendly voice:

'Of course I'll help you, Agnes, I've already told you, haven't I? Tell me, have you been through some very difficult things lately?'

'My father's death and later, my mother's,' she answe-

212

red immediately. Then she reflected: 'And… I had a terrible confrontation with René a couple of years ago. There wasn't even a clear cause, except perhaps for my infidelity many years ago. I would've thought that it was all resolved, but… he showed me his hatred. I know that he loves me, but he also hates me. He hates my…. hysteria, as he calls it. We used to fight each other with our hands and feet; I even started to take karate lessons to defend myself. But after that change, years ago, that was over. He had the power and no longer had to fight. I don't know if he felt that power disappear – we've never spoken about the incident again. There must've been a cause, but I must've forgotten it… in any case he's beaten me. I always thought it was exciting, such a physical power struggle between a man and a woman. But at that moment, when that fantasy became reality, I was very scared. I forgot my karate and it was really very bad…. Since then, nothing's happened since, I don't have such a big mouth anymore… and I don't beat the children anymore. I used to do that often - it seemed useful in raising them - and I also let go of myself, see what I mean? René ignored me for a week, while I walked around like a cripple. I didn't dare to say anything… and gradually everything returned to normal.'

Johannes was baffled; she could see that.

'Did he – have you never talked it over?' he asked.

She shook her head.

'He always says: the only therapy for hysteria is a bucket of cold water on the head, or a firm beating. He's had to endure a lot as a psychiatrist, and can't do anything; he has to remain calm. Perhaps he's applied that therapy at home, or it was still just his retaliation for wounded pride, I really don't know.'

'How can you just go on living like that? Sitting at the same table together, sleeping together....'

'I already had my heart problems; they didn't originate because of it.'

'In any case, this has to be talked through, that's clear. Are there any other things?'

'At work, I experience a lot of stress, you know what I mean. And four children is a lot, although I have good help. I'm a woman of whom a lot is expected, at least by the outside world. I enjoy life, Johannes, its luxury and beauty... I know that I'm a difficult person, and not very friendly. I think that everything is beautiful, except people. They are stupid, weak and ugly. Nobody matches Agnes.' She smiled. 'That's nonsense... I know better now – and at the same time I still don't. The master says that I'm full of fear-'

'The master?'

'Your friend, the Indian man. I met him and he took me to his meditation room. I thought it was scary. I'm normally not afraid at all. Do you think that I'm the type who's easily frightened, such a weasel?'

'You're good at denying it, but he *is* right of course. He sees everything – well, at least, a lot.'

'What now?'

'Come with me to my medical office at the clinic; I'll examine you and do an ECG etc.'

She walked with him through the park to a building situated lower down. It was busy there, a lot busier than in the main building.

'The clinic is packed the whole year through... and also outside the season. We didn't think that the people here would give us their trust. We've grown to become a kind of district hospital in a short time, with a lot of acute problems. Fortunately, next to Eva, my wife, who does the alternative therapy, I have my right-hand man from Amsterdam with me. He catches everything. Without him, I wouldn't know what to do.'

He opened the door to his room. She felt a strong emotion; the interior of the room touched her like he touched her. You saw his devotion in everything, his care, his ability.

He did the physical examination as carefully and meticulously as an assistant doctor who still has much to learn. Eventually, he connected the ECG device and took an ECG. While she got dressed, he looked at it, and his face was serious when she resumed her place at his desk again. He looked up.

'During the examination everything seemed fine.' He got up with the ECG in his hand and showed it to her. 'But look, Agnes. Here is an old frontal infarct... and there are indications of ischemia, without tension but already visible.'

He put his arm around her shoulders, as if he wanted to protect her against the stroke that was inflicted upon her. 'It's very disappointing, you see?'

She hunched over.

The grand Agnes was gone. Surgery and then maybe ten

215

years… if everything went well. Death had stationed itself at a visible distance; she would never *not* see it anymore.

'What would you do, Johannes, if you had something like this? Tell me what *you* would do?'

'The question is: is every therapy justified if it lengthens life? Is it even allowed in the light of eternity? That's an ethical question, not a purely medical one. Nowadays, medical science works with protocols, you know that. If this is wrong, you do this, if that is wrong, you do that. You will say: euthanasia shows that we are not only busy increasing life spans. No, *quality* of life plays a role there. But those qualitative processes, we only have knowledge of them in the roughest way. Happiness or unhappiness, pain, suffering or wellbeing… those are the qualities that we know of. But we have no sense for the finer quality. Is surgery that lengthens life – while that life may restore happiness and well-being – always qualitatively justified in the finer sense? Do we have the same psychological and spiritual possibilities afterwards as we had before? There is no measuring equipment for that. Such questions of course also apply to aggressive chemical therapies. I can't prove to current medical science that severe qualitative damage does occur, however fine. Some interventions release patients, others enchain them. I could prove that, but scientists would have to be prepared to think the thing through from alpha to omega. Yet they drop out, let's say, at beta already. They want visible evidence, not cognitive evidence, which does accompany observation, but which goes inside each thinker individually. For you, there are two paths: on the external path, you will let the doctors do a catheterisation, and we shall be afraid of what will be the outcome of that: advice to undergo surgery. You'll have that if it is necessary; you'll revalidate your life and live on fitter, until the same problem occurs again, and we'll see what to do then. Who knows how far science will have advanced by then? The internal path is one of far-reaching self- knowledge, a path of practice that asks for thorough input every day: being willing to observe yourself honestly, from a metamorphosing conscience. Cures help, but the most important thing is the 'internal hygiene'. If you ask me what I would do, it's an impossible question, because I have already been following that path for years now, without disease being the stimulus for it. I wouldn't have surgery, because I see through the qualitative, psychological-spiritual consequences of it, as they would be exclusively for *me* as an individual. Agnes, there'll be a time when I'll be confronted with my responsibility for these words, a time when official medical protocols will be obligatory, when the doctor who doesn't stick to them will be judged a criminal. That's why I am here - regarded as an unimportant, meaningless doctor by the medical establishment - in the mountains; I cannot submit myself to protocols because I see through what they are essentially.'

'And if I die of a heart attack within three years, while I could've lived on for many years if I had surgery?'

'You asked me what *I* would do. Understand me well, I don't advise you to abandon surgery, it wouldn't even occur to me. Still, it's not only the quantity – the number of years – that's the criterion. If you have the ability of the soul and

217

the spirit to develop themselves – that is, *quality* – three years can be more than ten years.'

'My God, Johannes! What should I do!?'

'I must reflect on that. I'd like you to talk to the master again. Ask him what he thinks of it.'

This time the master welcomed her into his room in the main building. He sat with his back to the window and got up when she entered. Here there were no carpets, it was light, the room was well-furnished, and the window had a view onto the park. He smiled warmly. Now he was not a dangerous lion of whom she had to be afraid; he was a nice, dark gentleman....

'Sit down,' he invited her. 'This time your friend has asked me several questions. The doctor, your Johannes, gives his diagnosis from the light of the spirit; the master who is sitting in front of you feels the processes of your body....' He was silent for a while. She felt nervous. Did she have to believe all this?

'You know....' he said, pondering, 'it is not all as bad as it looks on an ECG. One only registers a little part of what is in fact happening. An old infarct... yes, of course. Oxygen shortage to the heart muscle? Sure. But the cause lies much more in the dynamics of the blood vessels than in a bad condition of the vascular wall, at least in your case it does.' He bent forward a little and said: 'You are a very sensitive person, Agnes, even though you don't want to know it. You have rationalised away your fears and sensibility with it. You are determined to get everything possible from life and not be slowed down by all kinds of weaknesses. That

218

is understandable, when I observe your being, the way it is outside the small boundaries of life, You have far too much strength for such great sensitivity… yet still your will is weak. Your self-will is strong, but your actual willpower is not. Such an imbalance seizes the body, year in, year out. In your case it is still primarily *dynamic*, child. No clogged blood-vessels, but spasms. Fear. You are very scared, perhaps most of all of yourself, of who you are in essence.'

She sighed. All faith stops here, she thought. It makes no sense to argue about faith when you feel the truth in every sentence. She said:

'I'm a *bad* person, master. Do you see that I'm a *bad* person? Do you see that too?'

'People who say that they are bad are *lazy*.'

'I work very hard! I have a tough job as a surgeon, at home a husband and four children, fitness class twice a week and I don't know what more!' she exclaimed indignantly.

'You like to do all that; that is no effort. But when you have to do something that is asked of you, you start to resist, like a little child that does not want to help with the dishes. I am talking about an inner laziness, almost complete passivity. The only activity is inner resistance – and that hollows out the will; it makes one weaker and weaker.'

'I am strong, master!'

'That is the *maya* of the tangible. You have a beautiful, well-trained and maintained body. But you cannot endure anything.'

She got angrier and angrier.

'I was given a beating and I didn't make a sound; even

afterwards I didn't complain but just put up with it.'

'That seems kind of dumb to me. I assume that it was a *human being* who hit you?'

She nodded.

'Then you should have researched the motive. Laziness and fear, Agnes, that is what it is about.'

He just sat there quietly, uttering these crude insults. Why didn't she just get up? Because it was true… she said:

'Still I'm a bad person, lazy or not, anxious or not, I'm bad. I like to look down on people, with venom, begrudge anyone else's happiness and continue like that. When my daughter begs me to explain to me why she did this or that, I slap her – and I like it.' She was provoking him. 'I frighten the living daylight out of my co-students by giving them tedious assignments, I'm deliberately unfriendly – and the whole world can go to hell, as far as I'm concerned! With you and Johannes and the whole mess along with it!'

She burst into tears, angry and desperate at the same time. The cramp in her chest started again. He saw it, got up and rubbed between her shoulders with his hand. The pain went away; he put his other hand softly on the back of her head and pushed her a little bit forward; a feeling of well-being came from these soft hands.

'Tell me honestly, Agnes. Is that the only thing that you can tell me about yourself? Is there no beam of light anywhere? Something good, a little virtue in that childlike heart of yours? Mmm?'

She sobbed, uncontrolled. She wanted to be that child, that little girl on daddy's lap, with a whole life in front of her, unspoiled…. He caressed and comforted her, until she settled down. Her make-up was smudged, there were stains on her blouse, her hair was out of order. She blew her nose in the handkerchief of the master and stuttered:

'Yes... there is something, master. It's that I feel regret. Such regret. And already for such a long time now... who wants to be hard and hated, like I am? I have always felt inferior, inferior to my sister, my father, my mother. Inferior to René... to my children. My only motive is self-glorification, because I'm a zero, a nothing. Agnes is beautiful, jealous and lazy. She gets buckets of tar poured on her and that is exactly what she deserves. But I don't want to be a good girl; you don't achieve anything in the world by being good, not a whistle. So, do I want to change? No!' She looked up into the faithful brown eyes of the wise man. 'And still... I feel regret. Do you see the chaos, master? The paradoxes? I regret *everything*, who I am, what I've done. I've done a lot of bad things, injustice, lying, cheating – and with pleasure. And still also with regret. But who do I need to turn to for forgiveness? To the priest in the confessional? To Johannes? Maria? René? When you show regret, you're weak; you're truly a zero. I've felt remorse that I never really spoke with daddy. When he was dead, I almost lost my mind with remorse. Johannes said: *Feel* the powerlessness. And what've I done? To forget the pain, I've screamed even louder than I already did.'

'Regret only makes sense when you can feel it with inner peace. When you are devoured by it, it is exactly the same egoism that is tormenting you as in the sin. Regret must make you see how imperfect you still are – and you must endure it peacefully. Might there be another little virtue in this angry Agnes?'

She felt like a child, a pre-schooler. Opposite her was a wizard, well-meaning or not. She did not have to confess her sins here, but her virtues – if she had them.

'Is longing a virtue, master? Everything inside me is longing. I search within myself and all means are allowed. I grasp in the nothingness, but it's bottomless. I need the outside world to confirm that I exist, but *what* exactly exists, I don't know. I would want to *be,* just like that, like my twin sister; she needs nothing or nobody to be able to say: 'I am!' Yes master, I am frightened. Frightened of myself, of emptiness, of transience, of death. I have a beautiful house, expensive clothes and a sports car, jewellery and a big bank account. Everything to prove that Agnes exists. But when I'm dead, that will still be here... so it's not Agnes at all, it's just products. Longing, master. For *being*. I don't exist; my environment makes me exist!'

She felt compassion; she saw it in his eyes, on his face. He said:

'Longing is a virtue, Agnes. From my Buddhism I learned – and taught – that all longing brings suffering. Longing is the greatest source of sorrow, and must be put away systematically. Then I met Johannes and I started longing intensely. I longed to understand how he could be like I saw he was; I longed for his friendship, his closeness, for a realization of *being* here and now, on earth, and not in Nirvana. Everything a man can and *may* long for, is here with us on earth. We just lack a sense to observe that great happiness. Yes, Agnes, longing is a virtue, perhaps the greatest and most inescapable virtue of all time.'

'What do I have to do?' she asked desperately.

'Search yourself, Agnes – but search for yourself within. Everyone knows that you exist now; you don't have to prove that to us anymore. You still think: I'm in a fairy tale here. Well then: go in there, along inner paths, in search of yourself. Only finding yourself can cure you from your selfishness. Selfishness is desire for the self; it stops when you have found yourself. Seek the light which is only to be found where the sun sets, child. Physical light holds you back from being able to see the light within.'

He let her go, and her longing was greater than ever, but in front of her there was nothing, absolutely nothing. She was in front of absolute emptiness, the abyss of existence – she was in front of the abyss of her own being.

Communicative action is action based upon this deliberative process, where two or more individuals interact and coordinate their action based upon agreed interpretations of the situation.

Jürgen Habermas

Human affairs are often crossed pathways that faith has cleared. Jean wanted to come along so badly to that wonderful institution in the mountains, to Johannes… and had to let Maria go by herself because an important case was coming up. He would join her several days later. Maria took the train. At the station, Maria wanted to take a cab, but to her surprise, Johannes himself was at the platform. He hugged her like a good, old friend, took her bag and showed her to his car.

'I hope that you have no objections to staying at my house, Maria. We have a lot of room – and now you've finally come, I want to have you close to me!'

He was like the sun again, which lightens and warms. It made her a little shy.

'Did you have a pleasant journey?'

'Long, but quiet. Jean's coming on Monday by car. How was Agnes?'

He was silent and thoughtful while he drove around the hairpin bends. Just when she started to think that he had not heard her, he answered.

'When the heart is in despair, it is hellish for the soul'. The opening words of Parzival really apply to her. If she only just wanted to be that sweet, innocent child that she still is

225

in the depths of her soul... all that unnecessary uproar....
How's your relationship with her?'

'We trust each other very much, of course, I mean, we're at ease with each other, even though we don't talk a lot. We don't have much in common. She only talks to me when she's in trouble, so we don't see each other often. And Jean doesn't feel like getting in contact with her and René; he's too puritanical; he becomes sick of them. She's always acted as if she was far above me – at least in a certain way. She's made much more of her life, she thinks. On the other hand, she puts me on such a high pedestal that we can't see each other anymore. I don't really see that innocent child. She's somebody who is mostly a burden. René is pretty balanced and I admire him for his patience with her – although he also sometimes loses it.'

Because of the conversation, she did not see much of the landscape. Suddenly, they were driving into a plain, a valley at a great height, between impressive peaks.

'This is pretty different from Amsterdam,' she mumbled.

'I really miss that old trusty city built on piles... But for the path to the spirit this is a blissful environment. I'm looking forward to introducing you to everyone.'

He drove the car to the front of a garage of a large, newly-built chalet. She felt outside reality. She was walking alongside a friend whom she barely knew, in a country where she had never been before and yet everything was somehow familiar. A life of longing was behind her - longing for a truth that can stretch outside space and time, to eternity, to true friendship. She had worked for ten years and had waited, after she had seen the direction in which she had

226

to go. Now she was at the doorstep of the satisfaction of her longing... which would incite constant new longings.

To the left of the hall were the living rooms, and to the right, a study and a spacious guest room with folding-doors to a private garden.

'I'll leave you to yourself now,' he said. 'Shall I set the table for lunch? The children are at school; my wife's at the clinic. You'll meet them tonight.'

She nodded. He closed the door, and she was alone. She sat on the bed. Nothing can be within except what has been taken in by the senses. It truly seemed to be like that... until you get to know what really comes from *you*, from your own innate being, beyond all sensory impressions. Not dependent on experience from your upbringing or your environment. Completely *innate*. The *way* in which you take in all these impressions, order them, understand, remember or forget them is as individual as that being who you refer to as 'I'. 'That comes from the genes and is based on the individual characteristics of the body,' says the materialist. But that is a hasty answer, based on no deep research - for it is precisely that specific way of handling the sensory impressions that is especially *not* physical. You can learn to observe that, if you examine within yourself the non-sensory part of the cognitive process over and over again. It gradually becomes an observable activity – and in the observation it becomes self-evident that the body does not participate in this; it does not enter into the process *at all*. The process is an area to itself, like a second body, universal but completely individual, it is an almost *exciting* experience that really makes you tremble...

227

Here, now, it was as if she had come to a temple where a high priest was living… in our modern, down-to-earth times it was just Johannes in his chalet in the mountains. This latter view was that of the anxious mind: for modern man is terribly frightened of the heights and depths of the spirit, certainly when they manifest in a fellow being. Maria had no difficulties with it; she saw through the *maya* of sense appearances that she was in a temple, where a high priest lived and worked, where he had received the initiation and was giving his all now to pass it on to other people. She saw Johannes without that veil of the body in which he lived, in the profession that he was practising. She saw him in the present, but she also saw behind him to what he had once been.

They sat opposite each other at the kitchen table. Everywhere in the house it was light and clean, spacious and simple.

'I'm very… grateful that you have so much time for me' she said shyly

He smiled.

'I told you already that in a couple of weeks the summer commotion will begin. For many people it's an exquisite holiday with a tinge of spirituality. They seek peace, diet-cures, meditation-cures, massage-cures. They get upset if they have to become internally active. A singing recital, a lecture about philosophy… that's OK, that's a normal part of a cultural upbringing. But to very, very few people Maria, is it anything really serious. I'm here for them, but the rest is a kind of a torture. All kind, benevolent people with

228

talents and weaknesses, but without any notion of what our time is asking of us. Everything will be okay naturally, they think, if you're only able to observe and listen well. They come here and tell me that I'm working in a way that is too intellectual and rational and that they know a much better path for me.'

Maria was appalled and noticed that her hands had become clammy. She asked, baffled:

'What do you do with that? How do you handle it? '

He shook his head.

'I don't. Nothing. The serious few get ninety-nine percent of my attention. The rest get one percent; they have to share that. Sometimes even that's too much.'

'But... you, with your talents, your power, your cup of overflowing love ... Johannes! As a professor at least, you had hundreds of pupils who could learn from you....'

'That was no longer possible, it really wasn't. I always had to keep my profession and my actual *being* artificially separate. You die from that eventually, Maria. I 'sinned' consciously, day and night, against my spiritual path. Not because I saw nothing good in medical science as it is, but because I could no longer work from out of my being, my skill, my development. Here, I can give myself completely, or I hold back consciously, but I can at least *be*, and openly. This visit from you, Maria, makes all the opposition, all the daily nonsense, unimportant. I gave you one direction, at your father's grave, and you've got everything out of it that you could, in solitude, with all your strength and in complete freedom, led by nothing other than what you have within you. Now you're here and I know that, spiritually, you are completely by my side. Without any reserve. Not as a student, but as a partner in distress, a comrade, a colleague.'

'From the outside it may look like agreement, based on mutual faith. But in fact, nothing could be further from the truth. The tones in a chord aren't in harmony with each other because of their equal orientation, but because of the harmonic differences between them. You and I... Johannes... have no untested convictions. They are based on assuming something. In us, the spirit speaks, as objectively tangible as the voice of another man. That the same spirit keeps you and me in accord is self-evident.'

'If you're not too tired, I'd like to show you around and introduce you to my friend, the master.'

He cleared the table, and as he did so, she observed his movements. She saw a *human being* in him, but greater than all others, perhaps also older than all others. Someone who has experienced human development through all his lives, but soft and tender, full of respect, in spite of all his inner experience. In this time of computers and satellites, leaders withdraw into the mountains, to give all their greatness to the very few who are truly serious...

She was tired, but said:

'My fatigue will definitely disappear....'

He put on his suit jacket and walked outside with her, where the spring sun gave quite some warmth already. She walked alongside him on a path through the fields. In the distance there was a large building, the main building. Walking beside him, she felt a distant past resounding, in which she had also walked beside him. He was physically an attractive man, smooth and handsome, with quite a flair in social intercourse. This man next to her could not be described in such categories. He was not an individuality in a physical body...

with him everything was one, a consonance of beauty, wisdom and power, while that unity was maintained consciously by himself from a complete autonomy of those three become perfect beings in the soul: thinking, feeling and willing. She wanted to shout at the walkers who were passing them and greeting them politely: Wake up! Realise what kind of man is walking here, who is greeting you here, be aware how special it is to be able to meet such a man like this in these modern times. Don't walk by regardless. You don't have to admire him; just realise your good fortune and accept with all your power what he is offering you! Don't wait to recognize him until he is dead!

'After my studies, Maria, I clearly observed how the modern methods of raising and educating children kill the soul. The soul becomes a pale, cold corpse; you look at the white sun with dead eyes and you analyze its light as consisting of certain frequencies. I lived with the loss until I met the master. He threw me back into the thoughts of my lost youth and it was tempting to follow him. But I wasn't allowed just to go back; I had to go through death. You've been down the same road, you've suffered from the limitations of sensory observations. You *came to know* that it's just image, a veil *in front of* a different reality, but you didn't succeed in transforming that knowledge into action.

I've walked the path from thinking to observation; *you've* walked the path from the senses to concepts. Here, half-way, we meet each other. I want to ask you to describe to me in as much detail as possible how your path has been. Tomorrow, the day after tomorrow, whenever you want.'

'Tomorrow, Johannes.'

She had seen the institute, had shaken the hand of a couple of employees and now they were walking further down the path, in the direction of an older chalet, all the time on the other side of the institute's property.

'He's expecting us and is looking forward to meeting us. Agnes has met him a couple of times, she was afraid of him.'

'Afraid?'

'He possesses an elementary power, like a storm and thunder. He can also shine like the sun, but he's shown his thunder and lightning to her. When you see him, you'll understand how his being interested me at a time when *my* being was exiled in abstraction, in science. Besides having great empathy, he truly is a sweet man, with a tender and intimate heart.'

In the distance, on the terrace, she saw a small, dark figure waving at them.

'He's so fond of people!' Johannes said softly. 'And he's so often disappointed!'

He was small and quite heavily-built, with a large head and thick grey-black hair, beautiful brown eyes full of longing and unlikely white teeth. He was wearing black trousers and a black shirt, which made him look like a priest. He shook her hand cordially and exclaimed:

'Maria! The same name as my life companion. Maria. She proclaims herself the head of the household and is in a meeting with the financial director, Dr. Stern, at the moment. But you will meet her later, Maria! You do not look like your twin sister at all, in no respect at all. Mmm... except the radiation, that is purely physical in Agnes and in you it is purely spiritual. Come sit with me, Maria! You are a long-expected guest.'

They sat down on the terrace, while the master carefully put a serving tray with glasses, bottles and a teapot on the table.

'In the past I was not able to brew a cup of tea. Than I came as a manservant to our esteemed man here, the professor-'

'Manservant?' Johannes called out laughing. He turned to Maria and explained: 'He cared for our children when they were very small and Eva had to graduate.'

'Anyway, now I can even prepare a good meal. Would you like tea, or some soda, Maria?'

She drank her tea and looked out from the terrace to the other side of the valley, where the high peaks reflected the sunlight with a regal brilliance. She gave a deep sigh. She had left her father's beloved country, the land of apple-trees... and was in an area full of impressive contrasts now – even in the people! The master grinned.

'You have a great resilience. Such a long trip and now already here, on the terrace with the old master. You are not easily confused.'

'Were you trying to confuse me?' she asked in surprise.

'Of course not! But I know the effect of the master, child. Few can cope with it, because honest self-knowledge is lacking. One does not become aware of what I see, do you understand? But to you, that is nothing new, you know yourself. Furthermore, I see your great beauty, child. Great beauty.'

She kept silent. Well, she felt his power, of course. But she did not feel fear, she felt trust.

'Are you here to help us?' he asked earnestly.

'I don't know yet, master. I wanted to come here for years, but life kept me from it. Now I could no longer hesitate and I immediately looked to contact Johannes. First, I want to talk to him and also to you, exchange thoughts, learn from you. I have my life at home, my husband, my children, even though they are adults. I want to join my powers with yours – but how is not yet clear to me.'

The master nodded warmly. He turned to Johannes.

'An exceptionally self-aware woman. Self-aware and very polite. She, Maria, is wisdom itself. Wisdom, Johannes, is, as you know, a woman. I do not want to say: *wisdom is woman*. That would be incorrect, many woman are definitely unwise. As a Buddhist, I have searched for what Maria represents: pure sensory observation, devoid of all thinking. You searched that too, but in your western way, by strengthening your thinking. She is neither East or West… I would like to hear from her how she has come this far.'

The man in the hills, the angel on her path, the ethereal Master, had removed all insecurity from her. He had given her an initiation, because of which she could endure wit-

234

hout effort the image that the master painted of her here. For what he said was completely *true*. She had worked on her own, just with the help of a couple of sentences, but with the 'Master of the West' as the light on her path. The discipline had been *her* free choice, and that freedom had been rewarded with gifts for which words still had to be invented. The master saw that without effort, Johannes *knew* it…. They expected something from her….

Only in the evening did Maria meet Eva. Johannes had shown her the clinic, but Eva was then at work in her office and he did not want to disturb her. Afterwards, Maria had rested for an hour and when she had left her room hesitantly she ran into her hostess in the hall.

She had often had cause to regret her shyness … during that physiology practicum for example, all those years ago. Johannes had been the ideal man for her and she had missed her chance. Now, she was suddenly standing in front of Eva and she knew: there is no coincidence in life; everything goes the way it is supposed to go. Of course Johannes had to wait for this woman, with whom he had spent so many lives in intimate relationship. She just saw that, in one sweeping glance. Eva was young and flexible, perhaps not yet forty years old, sweet and spontaneous, but with an inner calm that Maria had only seen in Johannes, and in no other person…. Just for a moment she almost felt inferior, old, ugly and insignificant. But Eva immediately dispelled that feeling by greeting her like a long-expected guest. Shivering, Maria followed her to the living room, where she also now met the three children, two boys of twelve and eleven years old and a nine year-old girl. After saying hello, the children left the room, and Maria remained behind with Eva.

'It seems a heavy life, your work and the three children….' she said clumsily. She had to struggle with her admiration for this woman who lived alongside Johannes.

Eva sat opposite her and said:

'I've always had a lot of energy, perhaps too much. Now it comes in handy. I do have a lot of help. Someone cooks for us, and the children also have to help. I still have the tendency to take care of everything, because they have to work hard at school. But Johannes always follows a straight line, you can't do anything about that, but I'm curious how that'll go with the children when they get to puberty. But you've also always worked besides your family life, haven't you, Maria?'

'That was a sideshow; everything was a sideshow, actually. My whole life was a 'sideshow' when I look back on it now.' She felt a powerful happiness in her heart and added: 'I am very happy that I am here now. Behind that 'sideshow' I see the perspective of reality in which daily life seems to become clearer and clearer.'

She felt understood and completely accepted as she was. Eva said, smiling:

'You're very different from your sister, Agnes. She forces you to respect her. I'm glad that I didn't meet her as head of the clinic or something. She has a great liking for Johannes, fortunately – and I think he has a hold over her.'

'She's miserable. We're very worried about her. But it's difficult to get through to her. She closes herself off too much.'

Again she felt how such conversations completely miss the point, how much one does a person wrong by them. They both knew very well who Agnes was and what was wrong with her, but the words did not at all express that. They were silent. Finally, Eva sighed deeply, looked at her with clear blue eyes and said:

'Agnes has driven a wedge between us. Well, actually I did that by starting to talk about her. How long will be you staying with us, Maria?'

'For two weeks I hope ....'

Eventually, she saw them together, Eva and Johannes. She was amazed at the tenderness that Johannes showed towards his wife; he seemed like another man next to her, as if he was only a loving husband, nothing else. She could imagine that you would come to love this woman, Eva, very, very much. She was so open, so natural, so devoted also. He was attentive, did not let her out of his eye for a second... between them there was no jealousy, no friction. There was harmony between two worlds, so different....

Deeply touched, she fell asleep, and was touched more intensely when she woke up. She was in a temple here, where one knew what life on earth really is. Today she would tell Johannes what her path had been since her meeting with him at her father's grave.

The house was completely silent again; the children were at school, Eva at work... only Johannes was sitting in the sunny kitchen at the table. He had a medical office in the main building, a doctor's office at the clinic and at home a study – but he was waiting for her in the kitchen. Breakfast was ready and to her joy he stayed with her. 'It seems as if I'm always free,' he grinned. 'but I've postponed all my work until a further date. For me it is party time, now that you are here... I don't want to miss one hour with you. When Jean arrives later, things will be different....'

She looked up and asked:

'How do you deal with that? With jealousy in your development?'

His eyes were soft and blue. He answered, reflectively:

'It's the greatest problem in the life of a spiritual seeker. One has to deal with it all the time; it reveals itself at every possible turn. The most common form is mockery and outright rejection. But jealousy can also be turned into something good if it leads the other to a great commitment to achieve the same degree of development too. Real jealousy is based on laziness: one wants what the other has, but without having to commit oneself. There's also sincere sorrow about one's own 'lack', whatever it may be. Sincere sorrow can lead to great activity and commitment. I've never met Jean, but he seems to me to be someone of the second sort, someone with a great inner striving and desire and astonishment at the ease with which *you* make progress.'

She felt tears in her eyes, grief in her throat... Johannes understood so much and his understanding comforted her.

Jean would definitely like him.

'Thank you,' she said softly.

'I remember how alienated I felt during my studies, Johannes. As for the content, I learned more and more about the external form and function of the body, but I had the feeling that I was losing the *human being*, which I felt I'd known intuitively and completely, in a childlike sort of way. My father called my knowledge 'expertise' and he comforted me with the thought that I simply had the task to acquire that knowledge and lose the living human being – for a while, according to him. I was raised very religiously, intimately Catholic, and that really suited me. That heartfelt religious feeling, the feeling to be with 'Our Dear Lord' – I still think that that's a deeply touching name – disappeared at the same time with my original, but vague, human knowledge. I see a great similarity in that to your experience of the death of the soul. I haven't experienced it as distinctly as you, but it's the same thing in nature. I've read Novalis for quite some time, because my father thought I lacked romanticism. Then I got to know love, years later. Jean's an almost perfect lover; he knows how to keep romance alive through the years. He's an artist of living in ordinary life. He has everything at his disposal for that; a nice face, a good body, a clear mind, sensitive feelings, a talent for business and so on. Thanks to him I got to know ordinary life and learned to love it. Actually, there was nothing left to wish for. We also had two healthy, lovely children, who only had the usual kind of little problems. But still, dissatisfaction returned when I got more spare time. Meeting you was a turning point in my life. It must be like that for many people, Johannes. You do honour to your name; you summon people: 'Convert, I am the voice of one calling in the wilderness!' Only one who is deaf or disobedient will not hear that call. You've shown me the path very clearly; however, I had to walk it differently from you, because my point of view was different.

I've asked myself the questions that the Master asked you in the chapel:

'What is your greatest talent?'

When you ask yourself that question intensively, without pride and without feeling low, you already gain a lot of self-knowledge, even though it's still just as abstract as any other knowledge. I've had to search; I didn't have the answer ready immediately, like you. At first, I thought my answer to that question was compassion, empathy. That's certainly very strong in me, but it's a virtue, not a talent. I have a talent in observing, mainly in *seeing*. I've always had that, an eye for details, but also for light, colours, shapes.... The symbol of my talent is the apple tree in my parents' garden. There were a lot of apple trees there, but there was one with a stump beneath it, where my father and I always had our conversations. Stronger than the words, I remember the images, the wrinkles in his face, the drawing in his iris, his soul shining in his eyes... the beetle in the grass, the rusty spot on the chair in the garden... my whole youth comes to life in those images. I can see in a human being how his skin is, fresh or pale, powerful or withered. I have a talent to see that without jumping to conclusions, just to see it and let it affect me. Because of my 'scholarship' I left

240

that world somewhat; it became more colourless, poorer and more vague because of it.

'What is your greatest obstacle?'

My answer to that question is the same as *your* answer: my mental knowledge, yes, even the *function* of the mind. Which analyzes and combines but makes the world of images into a plan. I still see as sharply as before, my observation is undiminished with regard to my childhood, but the quality has almost completely left it, the eye of the artist has died.

'What is the greatest riddle?'

I've always lived with the question: is there more in the soul than what is taken in by the senses? That 'more' would convince me of an existence outside the body, before birth, after death. As far as I could 'see', I didn't find anything within me that did *not* come from the senses. And yet I still had a strong belief in God, in Christ. That was my riddle.

'What touches you the most?'

I could soon answer that one: death. It touches every human being. But I had to look deeper; my sorrow has some different nuances to it. My answer was: suffering. Suffering touches me the most, and my virtue also blossoms from that - in compassion. That suffering can originate from death but also from so many different causes. Suffering... touches me the most.

I asked the Master in the chapel, internally, as it were, who I of course did not meet myself:

What task results for me from this? Can I find an answer in the same way that the answer arose for Johannes from those four questions? Then I should be able to fathom what touches me the most – suffering – with my greatest talent – observing in images – and I would solve the riddle – is there more in the soul than what comes from the senses? – and conquer my greatest obstacle – the mind. I wrestled with all this, Johannes... not for days or weeks, but for years.'

'You're tired, Maria. Exhausted. I think that your story is breathtaking, but I want you to remain energetic.... We'll take a long break and continue this afternoon.'

She agreed unwillingly. He would go to work and she would have to miss him. But he said:

'If you'd like, we can walk down the hill to the village and have lunch there. It will do you good, a walk in the spring air. You'll see wildflowers that you've never seen before... and perhaps even an apple tree!'

'I've done research to see if I could pierce through with my greatest talent to what touches me the most...: I've tried to observe suffering. In my work I have little to do with that; little children, whom we examine in preventive medicine, show little sign of suffering. But I've experienced that *suffering* and passivity are almost the same; even the words correspond, while 'passion' also has the meaning of ardour, which makes an active impression at first. Nevertheless, it isn't so; suffering and passivity are the same. For Buddhism teaches that suffering comes from desire... ardour is indeed excitement, but passive. Naturally, passivity can be *forced*; one experiences that with physical suffering. Where can one observe *suffering* most distinctly? In the Stations of the Cross. Whether you believe it or not – and I've believed it

242

already my whole life – in the Stations of the Cross one sees suffering that exceeds all possible human suffering: suffering despite perfect innocence, in a freely chosen passivity, a free surrender. I was walking with Jean in the Eiffel region once, and we came through a small village with a large monastery and a monastery church. Sankt Thomas it was called. We went into the church and as always, a holy mood came to me... there was nobody else there. I was struck by the colour, the colour red... I don't remember if it was the pillars or the walls.

I walked around and I saw an image of Christ on the cross on one of those pillars. But it wasn't an ordinary image.... In front of the cross there was a monk with outstretched arms who was taking his Lord down from the cross. '*Bernard de Clairvaux*' was written beneath it. That was the image of what I had to do, Johannes: *Knowledge from compassion.* I had to come to the point where I could bar all my knowledge so that I wouldn't let it slip into my observation any more, unnoticed.... I wanted to observe like an innocent child again, like I could remember vaguely, like my father still could in his old age. But he already said: it's not possible just like that, knowledge paralyzes your observation, but you can't remove it just like that, like you turn off the radio. I felt that I'd be able to solve the great riddle: if I was able to observe purely, out of a compassionate knowing, *Knowledge from compassion,* I would find what exceeds birth and death in that observation. The mind has to be silent, but consciousness must be more powerful than ever. Still, one has the common mixture of observation and thoughts to thank for being awake.

I had an enormous task in front of me: to wake up in a consciousness in which one is normally asleep... or to pursue a complete transformation of consciousness. In our present state of mind one cannot observe without thinking. You, Johannes, can do that because your thinking is so free, conscious and powerful; you can let it in consciously or bar it. The master is able to do it because he still has ancient abilities that we no longer have - and shouldn't strive for either, because we shouldn't go back to the past, but develop the abilities that are typical for western people... I'm able to do it now, after years of struggle, because my thinking has given way to a very strong internal activity - compassion. Actually, that is also thinking activity, but completely in surrender, without any fulfilment, and filled with respect. Like Bernard de Clairvaux releases the Lord from the cross with outstretched arms... I pierce through, *from* myself, *into* the being of things. No-one should believe that one can undertake such a thing without committing one's whole being to it. It isn't a path only of glory or grace. I have stood before the meekness of my own mind like Parzival, before the Amfortas in me. I didn't know what to do, until I was touched by intense compassion, awakened by the image of the Pietà, the mother with her dead, innocent son.... Compassion gives power to true self-knowledge, to awakening the powers that slumber within, which are more than what comes from the senses.'

She was tired, exhausted. Johannes had a rare, great ability to understand; he understood every word that she had spoken. He understood because he actually already *knew*. One felt that he was entirely silent while he listened. What one said touched that silence, fell into it like seed in fertile soil. Nevertheless, she was tired, because she became aware so painfully that her words did not suffice to express her experiences. In speaking of them, she was a cripple, lame and blind. It was not speaking, it was stammering. Yet still she wanted to express clearly what she had experienced over the long years past. Tomorrow they would continue talking, and she would try again.

She missed Jean. He called her in the evening, but she missed his presence, his physical power, his tenderness. Johannes was a brother... Jean was her lover. She had always told him everything about her path, even if he showed jealousy. They lived together, internally and externally. She saw a similar fullness of living together in Eva and Johannes, but on an even higher level. Eva did not know jealousy; she was completely at one with Johannes' striving.

'Have you never felt any resistance?' she had asked Eva in the evening. Eva shook her head.

'I met him when his striving was already in full swing. He was at the peak of his career but he was also at the threshold of initiation. I knew very well what I was getting myself into, I had to fight for it. He was not looking for a wife at all. I was still studying, I was a grown-up child... the distance between us was enormous, and at the same time it just wasn't; there was absolutely no distance internally. During the day he was that successful professor and at night,

245

he studied the mediaeval Scholastic philosophy and practised rigorous logic, in thinking in well-considered concepts. He was rigorous and vigorous in everything – and there was I, rash and young. But yes, if I'd been more cautious, I would never have had the daring to enter his life. Now I just came walking in, time after time… until he also saw that we belong together. Yes, one time I resisted, completely unjustly, by the way. And he really didn't understand; it was not understandable. I felt then that it shouldn't happen again… for Johannes, it was no light matter. The children also have a holy respect for him too. When they go into the big wide world, they'll be surprised by all the injustice, mendacity and hostility between people. They haven't been raised with any of that.'

'No doubt they will draw power from their upbringing to become entirely themselves.'

'What have you *done* to achieve your ability to observe without thinking, but *with* the gift of compassion, Maria?'

They were sitting opposite each other at the kitchen table. She felt fit again and was determined to answer as clearly as possible.

'I read a lot, in order to get a complete understanding of what that complete metamorphosis of consciousness really is, which is described by the 'Master of the West'. At the same time, I explored the contents obtained with that transformed consciousness. Your books, Johannes, are a guide on the path of that metamorphosis. Nevertheless, I had the feeling that I was coming from the other side, although your path is so comprehensive that this other side is as natural to you as the side of the rigorous formation of concepts. 'Consciousness without a conscious object' – that's what has to be achieved, ultimately. As I said yesterday already, one can't achieve that without committing one's whole being to it or without being prepared to go into battle against the countervailing powers – the opponents against proper development who live within us as well as outside us. Since then, I've actually lived at a level of intensity I hadn't expected was possible.'

'That's your study, your preparation. Which practice have you done as meditation?'

She smiled. Johannes was keeping track well of what she was telling him. First study, then meditation, and finally both, fertilizing each other.

'The guiding sentences that you gave me, at my father's grave, have been my material for meditation. I've tried to fathom them, and besides that I have tried to hold them within me, in intense attention and surrender. Because of that, my thinking settled down into them and the sentences finally became an answer to my questions – all very slowly, in the course of years of rigorous practice. Before I started, I had moments of contact, of tender fulfilment, that made me shaky. Those moments became stronger and more frequent, but more and more only during meditation, and because of that I no longer became confused in my daily life. Finally, that inner touch became the force of compassion that replaces my thinking in moments of meditation, but also in moments of pure, sensory observation.'

'You haven't told me yet about the exercise in observation.'

247

'I quickly understood that sensory observation has a paralyzing effect on living thinking, but also gives one the possibility to be a free, self-aware person. One wants to lose the one, but not lose the other. How? One can understand something, Johannes, but that's still something other than being *able* to. One can understand that one has to be truthful, but that does not mean that one always *is*. So I understood that I had to learn to distinguish between pure observation and judgement, in order to be able to distinguish even more delicately later, namely, between observing and thinking that is associated with that, which is *not yet* judgement. I understood the difference, but I didn't live in it yet; I wasn't able yet to completely distinguish between observing and thinking. The concept was there in a couple of weeks, but the *ability* to be *able* to do what I had realized took many years to develop. One must keep meditating on what one has understood and keep asking for the strength that may transform the insight into a deed.'

'What does that *deed* then consist of, Maria?'

'I practised in continuous attention to the process of observation – I limited myself to the *seeing* – and thinking in and about that observation. One can also do that as an exercise, once a day. Later on, it becomes a habit. It doesn't have the effect of suppressing associative thinking just like that. One has to strive to observe consciously and think consciously. In order to develop the latter, I used the Categories of Aristotle. When I did an observation exercise, I just *strengthened* thinking with the help of these categories instead of suppressing it. But because thinking in concepts is naturally abstract and weak, powerless, my observation indeed became more conscious, but not more vivid. As I went on, towards whichever direction I aimed my inner attention, I continuously came up against abstract, lifeless, conceptual thinking. I experienced how the mind paralyzes the experience of the beauty of observation, but that sensory observation in turn paralyzes the vivacity of understanding. One must learn to keep both apart in order to have *both* fully engaged in observation. Meditatively, I started to pierce through the pure concepts that are given in the Categories. For example, when one reflects on the concept of 'quality' meditatively, one has a concept that does not have a sensory content, but *comprises* all sensory qualities. In addition, when observing, I tried just to *look*, with my eyes open, and to put aside all thinking, including the Categories. It doesn't work at first; one keeps thinking. It only works when one *has* pure, sense-free thinking *so* consciously that one can keep it *outside of* the observation. In sense-free concepts, in maintaining them, there is a powerful thinking-will, which is purely spiritual. But if you want to learn to *understand* that pure spirit, you must know its language. You get to know it through the inner effects that arise with an attentive sensory observation, *without* any thinking whatsoever. Complete attentive observation and an attentive experiencing of what moves internally: this is how one gets to know the language of the spirit. But nothing speaks itself, when inner peace and determination are not yet developed. So, meditation on the one hand and observation on the other hand mesh together; they strengthen each other because they are free from each other: thinking without sensory content and observation without thinking. So I found the answer to the riddle: the content of the mind comes in the first instance from the senses; the *activity* of thinking absolutely not. One can only find it when all influences from the senses - including echoes in the memory - are held back.

Jean called her to say that he was close to the institute and would be arriving in a minute. She had already been waiting for a while, in the sunshine, on a bench in the park. She walked towards the main entrance and saw him coming, in his sports car. He drove up to her feet, stopped with the car tyres screaming and jumped out of the car laughing. He hugged her and lifted her up in the air.

She was fifty years old but felt like she was eighteen.

'You look like a girl,' he greeted her.

She looked at him well. He was tired from the trip, but he wasn't a man in his fifties either. Love kept him young. Love...and their joint spiritual striving.

'Where is Johannes?' he asked with a smile.

'We're going to see him now,' she said.

She took his hand and walked inside with him, to Johannes....

*

To Agnes' astonishment, René was waiting for her at Schiphol. She wasn't used to that; they both went their own ways and met each other at home. She had her intense job in a man's world; he was still digging himself like a mole into the most diverse literature. She already saw him from a distance. He didn't look much like that dissatisfied, protesting, trendy pain-in-the-arse he used to be. He had gained weight, was a little bold… always dressed in an expensive jacket. Only the cigarette was still there. He actually had a beautiful head, René. Not handsome, but interesting, special. She felt a certain pride, that he was her partner. He had become a man with many qualities, musical, philosophical, understanding.

He took her in his arms and held her close for a while.

'I missed you,' he whispered. 'How was it with Johannes?'

He carried her bag. She grumbled:

'Difficult. He was not so nice at all. Severe and cool, that's what he was. And that friend of his, the Indian man, is a creep.'

René put his arm around her, smiling, and said:

'I talked to him, to Johannes. I thought he was kind, warm and committed. In the end his advice was: examination by the cardiologist and if his diagnosis is the same as Johannes', you can go there for a cure for a couple of months.'

She shivered and said mockingly:

'O, may I? How kind!'

He opened the door for her and helped her into the car. Unperturbed, he went on:

'Yes, you may. In the meantime you are no longer allowed to work and you must rest in the afternoon and walk and cycle a lot etc.'

He got in and drove backwards.

'Watch out!' she yelled. 'You'll hit a passer-by!'

He grinned.

'Mrs Director is back! When you are not around, I still don't have any accidents.'

'I do,' she squeaked. 'In a metaphorical sense, I do.'

She reached for his hand.

'I have got an assignment, René. A couple of them. I must talk to you.'

'Of course,' he said calmly. 'First, the children. They are waiting for you at home with cake.'

She could not imagine that they were happy that she had come home again. They must be putting on an act: 'Party for mama's return.'

But they hugged her one by one, which made her cry. The table was set festively and there was coffee and cake ready.

'That's not good for a heart patient,' she grumbled. She looked at the youngest, her ten year-old. Her daughter looked pale. Agnes took the little face in her hand, looked into her brown eyes and asked:

'What is wrong, little one, you look so pale!'

Big tears rolled out of the brown eyes, but she didn't say anything. Agnes pulled the girl towards her: see, she thought, it was terrible that her mother was back.

But suddenly the girl sobbed:

'I was so afraid, mommy... that you would stay there or that you would... die.'

She burst into tears again. How could a girl like this love such a bad mother? One that was always away and when at home, was always snappy. How many times had she slapped the girl's face in mere annoyance and impatience.... Nobody would miss such a mother! But the girl clung to

252

her. She felt the warm, tender body, she felt the attachment. She hugged the child like she had never done before. Johannes and that Indian man had made something happen! She suddenly seemed to have *feelings*. The cramp in her chest rose again; it suddenly seemed like physical sorrow. She sat down. Everyone was looking at her, René too.

'Come on, everyone!' she said uncomfortably. 'You will have me around so much, that you'll soon have had enough of it.'

René put on some music and poured the coffee.

'It's bad for me, coffee. And all that sweetness too,' she said.

He caressed her hair and said:

'Today we're celebrating. Enjoy it for once.'

The boys soon became impatient and started to tell jokes. She let it be; she felt at home. Here were five people who had missed her and were partying because she had come home again.

She sat with René in the library. Now it had to come out. He had put his books aside and looked at her expectantly. She threw her projectile immediately.

'Why did you hit me?'

She could not look at him, why not actually? It was just not possible. She heard him shift his position, he took his head in his hands and said:

'I… regret it very much, Agnes.' He reached out to her, which helped her to look at him. 'I am sorry, my love. I am very sorry.'

'You don't have to say that,' she said defensively. 'A bad

253

person like me deserves a beating. But I never understood the actual reason for it – and didn't dare to ask you.'

She pushed his hand away; there was something compelling in the gesture. He gave a deep sigh.

'Do you really not know why? I came home and you were standing there, in front of that little girl that you hugged so tightly this afternoon. She was about seven years old then and begged you to be allowed to explain why she made I don't know what kind of mistake. She really *begged*, do you understand? And what did you do? You took a swing and hit her left, right, left in the face. I could've strangled you then, Agnes! I walked away because I didn't want to shock the child even more with my own aggression. I hated you! Hated! I wanted to make you feel what that is, when you're being beaten. I just wanted to pay you back in the same coin. But when I'd hit you once, everything came up. Everything. I could've killed you. If I'd been younger, I would've killed you. Now there's some kind of caution in the background, a conscience, a reserve. I know very well what I've done, I regret it and I ask you to forgive me.'

'If only you'd said something,' she said, shivering. 'Why did you keep silent afterwards?'

'I was paralyzed, afraid to lose you, but also still mad. That you'd pushed me *that* far. I felt how there's a path away from the straight path, a path I could easily have gone along, Agnes. On that path I would've repeated this, over and over again. I would've forced you to submit completely. I didn't go down that path, very consciously. But I couldn't say another word. You were completely intimidated. You would've accepted another beating too, because you know that you were to blame. I know these processes, I have to deal with them every day. I'm sorry, Agnes!'

She collapsed, she put her head on her arms on the table. Tears dropped on the wood, wet her sleeves. What a mess… *what* a mess.

He got up and came towards her, lifted her up, pressed her against his chest. She sobbed. My God, my God… she did love him, she had always loved him. She also loved her four children, *four* children, his and hers, together. Daddy… if she had only confessed to him, talked to him. God, God, what a mess. She also loved Johannes so much…If this cramp would only stay away! 'Come on, love. Throw it all out. You are always so tough, so strong.'

He caressed her back, she relaxed a bit.

'Strong…' she sniggered. 'Strong! A greater weakling has yet to be born. Strong…? Everything is just show, exhibition. I am nothing, nobody. A hole, a big dark hole. Like a star, you know. It twinkles, but there's nothing. You shouldn't be sorry. Those smacks have at least brought some balance. So you've done something wrong once at last. It did shock me, René. I was startled, and I'm afraid of you. I've always been afraid of you, that it would happen once. But now I know how awful such a thing is.'

'That's why I'm so sorry. You mustn't put yourself down so much. You're a talented woman.'

'But not kind. Never kind.'

'Now you are.'

'I love you so much, all of you. Everyone. Even that scary master.' She sobbed her heart out. So this is love? Complete surrender to the positive, without exerting oneself, without barricades, without buckets, hot tar on the ramparts, without artillery? My God, what a mess....

Within two days René had managed to get an au pair via the internet. It was a German girl, who wanted to go to college in Holland but had to learn the language first for a year. She was given a nice room and in change for that she would do the ironing, the groceries, cooking and if necessary, baby-sit. In those same two days Agnes went to the cardiologist and she experienced the respect that a diagnosis from Professor Leven, although no longer practising, still received. She was put on the list for a catheterisation.

Suddenly, she had all the time in the world. She felt how she had always avoided being bored, how she had filled her life with activity so that she did not have time for contemplation. For she *was* only present in action – when she started being bored, she was confronted with nothingness. In that state of 'I am *not*' she started to long for René very much. It was new, this longing. She didn't want to lose him, but she also didn't like his presence very much. Now she was lonely, during the endless days waiting for surgery.

René left with the children every morning. In the afternoon he was often at home but had his office hours. At night he played the cello or studied in the library. She sat with him now, and he was sensitive enough to understand that she needed him. She knew very well that it was a sacrifice for him when he put his books aside, or his cello, to turn to her. But with a fatherly kindness he made that sacrifice again every night. She was like a kitten that lay on his book preventing him from studying... he let her take the place of his book and went on with his work as a psychiatrist with her in the evenings.

He leaned back and asked:

'And, Agnes? How was your day?'

She shrugged her shoulders.

'I'm depressed, I think. Perhaps I've always been depressed and suppressed it with my ambition. This chest pain really seems like sorrow, like a soul sorrow that has become physical.'

'What is that sorrow then, love?'

If he asked such understanding questions, the sorrow only increased unbearably. The tears came.

'You're so kind.' She wept. 'Remorse, I think it's remorse. When you go on proving yourself, you don't come round to that feeling.'

'Remorse is so senseless. You'd better try to make 'it' up. Whatever 'it' may be.'

'You know what it is – and it *is* not possible to make it up. And anyway, there're all kinds of vague things. As a child, I was already like that, and at that time there was not much to have remorse about. Small things, lies and so... and a Catholic upbringing naturally plays a big role in remorse. At least, there was the confession and the forgiving of sins, however much I mocked it at the time. But René... in the end, the human being dies, and then what? Will I be judged for all my sins? Or is there nothing...? I could almost wish that there is *nothing*. You've forgiven me, I know that, René. But God… has different standards, if he exists.'

'If I, small, imperfect human being that I am, have forgiven you, God will certainly do so too.'

'But not without punishment. That would be too easy, and also unjust. Maria lives her life like a saint, and her small mistakes would not be forgiven in the same way as my big mistakes. There must be a difference, a difference in punishment. That punishment will be different from sitting in the corner for an hour, or writing a hundred lines of punishment. If I have to die from a heart attack, now or in ten years – what is waiting for me then?'

René shook his head and said:

'You have stayed the same Agnes for fifty years. You can start any moment making it up instead of waiting in agony for the moment of punishment.'

'Make it up – to you?'

'Not to me. To the Judge. To God.'

'How?'

'By not staying that same Agnes. By changing, by bettering yourself.'

'That won't succeed anymore. I'm too old for that.'

'It's not about the result, but about the activity, about the attempt to change in itself.'

'And what about you? Are you doing that?'

'Am I the same René, who you met when you were twenty years old?'

She was silent, astonished. No, he had become a completely different man. She had thought that it had been life that had changed him so much – but life had hardly changed *her*. She was still that same Agnes, only older and with

258

more experience. She was waiting for the punishment; *that* would have to change her. She let life pass her by, she used it to shine, not to change herself or perfect herself through it.

She did not feel like that either. If that pain had not come, she would have been able to live on until death captured her. Now she had to suffer from her doubts about God, her fear of Him. If she had had a different father, she could have thrown God overboard as nonsense and renounced her faith. Eventually, she had done that and she thought that she had succeeded. But inside her, everything hurt, and she knew that it was doubt. If it were *true*, what her father had lived for… and he was *so* sure, that it *had* to be true… she wanted to ask him that, she wanted to talk to him about it, suddenly she knew. About her doubt, her fear that God existed, she knew that she would be judged.

René got up and took her in his arms. She smelled the tobacco; she knew him so well. He whispered:

'My love, it does not make sense to think the way you do now. You must make sure you reach an agreement *before* the judgement. Use your days to gain honesty with yourself. Not for me; I am satisfied with you, I love you, even if you just stay as Agnes. But *you* must face yourself. This is destroying you, you are not superficial enough to keep this up. I know you, Agnes. I know you so well.'

He made her cry again. Was there ever a time that she despised those who cry? She despised herself… and René said that it didn't make sense.

'What should I do then? Go to Yoga and breathe in and out?'

He took her chin in his hand, like she did to her children when she caught them.

'Don't mock,' he said, but kissed her wet eyes.

'What then? Read all your books?'

'Agnes! Don't mock, I say. Look at yourself, look at your own prejudices. Don't walk away from them, look at them without regret or guilt, just objectively like through somebody else's eyes.'

'You know very well what a terrible view that will be.'

He pulled her towards him again.

'Is reality less terrible when you don't want to see it?'

'I want to be with you, René. You're so peaceful, so wise, so understanding.'

'Do you think that God is less peaceful, wise and understanding?'

She shook her head.

'No. But more strict, more like Johannes. It's the way it is, you're not rejected but you do have to work hard, you can't come up with poor excuses or flattery.'

'You can do that with me?'

She giggled.

'We have the sex, don't we?'

'Do you think that's why I've stayed with you, Agnes? For the sex?'

She put her arms around his waist and said a little unsteadily:

'No. Yes… I don't know. Why did you stay, René? Because I am Maria's sister?'

'Agnes, Agnes… don't you have any self-esteem at all?'

'Tell me then?!'

260

He sat down and pulled her onto his lap.

'Once upon a time...' he began and told her the fairy tale about Mother Hulda.

'I am that girl with the tar, Maria's the one with the gold,' she said when he had finished.

'That's the easy explanation, the 'tar-explanation'. There's also a more difficult explanation, the 'gold-explanation': both girls are inside you, Agnes. In you, in Maria, in me, in everyone. I've learned to see the gold-Agnes more and more behind that tar-Agnes. I love her the most, I love her *more* than I love Maria. Really. If you would only see her yourself....'

'You did give her a good beating, that tar-Agnes!'

'I'm trying to make it up to you, sweetheart... by giving you *my* other side. I want you to feel how devoted I am to you.'

Again the tears came....

Haste, haste, haste. She was nothing but agitation. Peace gave her the shivers.... What was she running from? It all looked so perfect: a female surgeon, beautiful as well, a nice family, with four healthy children, wealth.... Everything came from agitation. She had to build up as much as possible externally in order not to feel the *void* inside her. *Horror vacui....* O, there was enough to experience inside, hate and love, excitement, jealousy, courtship and power. But all that is supported by the 'outside'; the cause is always external. Now there was little to experience, she had whole days of peace, endless hours to walk on the beach, look at the waves and the sky, follow the sea-gulls.... However, she had no internal life so she had a hard time becoming free of her thoughts. Naturally, she was scared of the future. What was going to become of her? She had decided to take the conventional route: catheterisation and perhaps surgery. After all, she was not Johannes, she had no grip on herself, not even on her thoughts and feelings, let alone the processes in her body. It had to be handled from the outside. If she didn't have surgery, it would actually be more difficult: she would have to work on herself after all. If cramps could be the cause of the severe ischemia of the heart muscle, she would have to learn to relax. She was actually only relaxed after making love; even in her sleep she was convulsive, according to René. Now, during her walk on the beach, she was still tense. Haste, everlasting impatience, even when there were no obligations. It even seemed to get worse in peacefulness. She stood still and put a tablet under her tongue. The pain ebbed, and it seemed as if the haste also became less. She looked around. It was June, but there was no life on the beach; it was cold and heavily clouded. René found it terrible that she went for such long walks on the beach on her own. If she had a dog with her.... She could imagine that... how she would be overcome by some guy, later her body would wash ashore. Oh... she had often had such nightmare images. She should walk back, especially hasty, always with death at her heels....

She called Johannes.

'You are right, I consist of fear. I make myself crazy. If I don't have to have surgery, I'll come to you this summer, like you offered. I'll come anyway, Johannes. Something has to change. And I absolutely don't know how.'

There was silence at the other end.

'Are you still there?' she asked, annoyed.

A laugh.

'Yes, yes. I was listening to what you were saying.'

'I haven't said anything for a long time.'

'Hmm. What're you doing with your days, in your spare time?'

'Being bored, waiting for René – he is very kind to me – walking on the beach.'

'Start reading something.'

'I don't have the peace of mind to do that.'

'You have a whole library at your disposal, I understand.'

She giggled.

'I haven't read a single book from it – well, perhaps one or two.'

'Don't you have an interest in anything?'

'No. I like the sea wind in my hair, the splashing water around my feet, the sound of the waves, the wind and the sea-gulls. What I *read* can't compete with that.'

'Read a fairy tale and form the images so strongly that you could almost see them, touch them, that they become *alive*.'

'I absolutely don't feel like that, Johannes! I'm not a child!'

'What're you coming here for, Agnes, if you reject eve-rything?'

'Are you starting again? You shouldn't be so strict, you must let me be free.'

'I can do that if you ask nothing of me. Now you're asking me for help, but you don't want it.'

'I *do* want it!'

'No, you want me to say what you like.'

'All right, all right. I'll read a fairy tale and try to see, smell, taste what I read. All right?'

Johannes sniggered.

'Now you are a good girl. Will you call me again, Agnes?'

'Okay. Bye, Johannes....'

The first thing that she discovered was how simplistically she actually read the story. She had no images to shape; she hadn't read well enough in order to do so. She started over again.

An unwanted, ex-soldier had nothing to live for anymore and went off into the woods. She imagined a modern soldier, with a camouflage uniform and helmet, all worn-out and with a despondent look on his face, a little bent-over, walking into the woods. A forest. High trees everywhere, wet leaves on the ground, fresh air. She had enough fantasy to make something beautiful of it. She tried to smell the wet leaves, see the slugs, feel the hopeless life of the soldier. And then... suddenly a little man appeared, but it was the devil. A small chap with nasty green eyes, a pointed chin and horns on his head, who knew a way out of this misery. But the soldier would have to work in hell for seven years first – imagine that, he would not be able to wash himself, comb his hair, cut his nails, blow his nose, wipe his tears. For seven years!

She tried to imagine the filth. What exactly did he have to do there? In order to imagine that, she had to read it again. She tried to imagine hell with pots with fire underneath them everywhere. The soldier had to keep the fires burning, he had to keep stirring them up, but he wasn't allowed to look inside them. Also, he had to keep hell clean and put the garbage outside the door. He does all that, but after a certain time he looks inside the pots anyway. Acquaintances of his are in there, his superiors in the army. He stirs up the fire nicely. Okay... she was not so ruthless after all, she could not go with that. Even if she found someone who had harmed her – to increase the heat even more was horrible! But well, she had to imagine it and she felt the pleasure of the soldier stirring the fire beneath his superiors. The devil was very content about it: the soldier was disobedient, but at least he did not have compassion. A devil can do something with that!

Agnes began to enjoy it.

She called Johannes again. If he had enough of her, he should say so.

'Yes, Agnes?'

'It's wonderful!' she said enthusiastically. 'Really nice. Everything goes well on earth when one connects to the devil. Good people go to heaven, bad people achieve anything they want on earth.'

Johannes grinned.

'Go ahead, I would say.'

'I was on my way. Until I met you. You're to blame for me putting a break on myself.'

He remained silent.

'Are you there?'

'Yes. We could act as if we'd never met.'

'Fool! 'Life in heaven' will last longer than struggling on earth, I guess. So I'd better be safe than sorry, or rather: I choose that uncertain eternity of yours.'

'How do you feel?'

'When I'm busy with this, I forget everything. But afterwards it's the same. Bad. What do I have to do now?'

'Repeat the same every day for a week. Form images with the same enthusiasm, the same effort.'

'*The same images?*' she asked in disgust.

'The same fairy tale. Test your fantasy.'

'What sense does that make?'

'That you forget yourself for once.'

'Thank you,' she said sourly. 'Is that all?'

Again she heard his laugh.

'No. Write down exactly what you experience. I am very curious.'

'Will my 'cure' be like this too, next summer?'

'Yes.'

She sighed.

'I'd love to take a bath and have massages and so on.'

'We shall see what is necessary.'

'All right. I'll do it. Bye... Johannes.'

We hear daily how homoeopathic medicinal potencies
are called mere dilutions,
when they are the very opposite,
i.e., a true opening up of the natural substances
bringing to light and revealing
the hidden specific medicinal powers contained within.[2]

Samuel Hahnemann (1755-1843)

Maria took Jean to see Johannes. A lot depended on this first meeting. Jean was an intuitive, talented man; first impressions were often a guideline for him. Johannes was in conversation, so they had to wait for a while, on a couch in the hall. A lady came out of the room and a little later, he was there, in the doorway.

Johannes.

It was as if she saw him for the first time, through the eyes of her lover. But she suddenly saw her lover very differently too. For there was no question of rivalry, now that they had finally met. They shook each other's hand firmly, and she thought that she saw emotion. The light of the sun and the earnestness of Saturn, she saw them in both of them, but in a different mix. She sat down, while Jean looked around peacefully.

'Here one can forget what kind of world we live in,' he sighed.

'That's a problem at the same time,' Johannes answered. 'We seclude ourselves, but we also want to be in the centre of life.'

---

[2]   Organon of medicine, §269

Using the polite form of 'You', Jean asked: 'Do You never regret that You left Amsterdam?'

Johannes looked serious:

'Let's not use the polite form. No, I can't possibly regret taking such a well thought-out decision. It was matured over years. But that doesn't mean that it is always easy, that I don't miss my work at the clinic, with patients and students. With all due respect to the innovations of education and medical practice … for me it became impossible to continue my leading role there. It was a choice between, on the one hand, the progress of spiritual development and, on the other hand, the fertilizing of external life with it.'

Jean asked:

'But they should go hand in hand, shouldn't they? Wouldn't it be awful if that weren't possible?'

'It isn't possible, believe me. I tried it for ten years and felt how my spiritual power was captured, immobilised, chained by the duties required in my position. Those duties can be interpreted less and less in freedom by moral intuition, and are more and more dictated from the 'upper hand' of the State.'

Maria watched the two men in silence. She saw how Jean reflected on Johannes' words and she experienced how special it was that Johannes could speak for once about… how he himself actually stood in life.

Jean nodded.

'Yes, I can imagine that very well. But … how is it here then?'

'Everything always goes differently from how you expect it to go,' Johannes said smiling. 'We didn't count on the small clinic that was opened here blossoming, but it was already too small here after a couple of years. Of course we had trouble with licences and so on, but that was solved eventually and there is more work to do here than we can handle, in fact. So I have a lot to do after all and I've relinquished a lot less of my work than I expected to. Here I have freedom in therapy; I'm not bound to protocols, at least for now. Besides that, we naturally have lively contacts with all kinds of spiritual seekers.'

'That sounds exhausting, Johannes!'

He laughed.

'Most of all, I love those people who seek their own way to the spirit and who then ask for occasional counselling perhaps. But mostly, relations are the other way round: they come here for counselling, but have little appetite to become active in inner life, to *work* themselves. The master already struggled with that, but he just established a very tight regime: take it or leave it. Given the freedom that simply is the fundament on which modern initiation is founded, we've abolished that regime. One gets to see people for who they are. There is an almost boundless revulsion from inner activity – and yet that's the very condition for inner development.'

'Is it hopeless?'

Johannes looked at Jean earnestly:

'I don't want to say that; I'm only describing what I meet. The inner life is filled with passive content from earliest childhood onwards. That's just the way it is. I search for the onset point in the modern adult; it can sometimes be almost impossible to find. How does the dreaming soul shake itself awake when the final waking up is such a painful process? Why would one make it hard when it can also be easy? What can entice and captivate a man who's learned to appreciate the luxury of being lazy? Well, I hope that you understand what I mean. The ancient path of initiation is no longer active, and the new one calls for powers that don't seem to exist yet.'

'But what about you? *You've* also grown up in our time and you *do* prefer inner activity. And Maria too… and I believe that I don't deny it either. Perhaps you can see something in that?'

Johannes shook his head.

'We long for it; we can't live when we don't awaken that activity in ourselves; we were born with that longing. There are few like us, Jean. People don't know that the source of all suffering is inner passivity. I truly feel sorry for all those suffering people, do you understand? The solution is there to be taken

, but where is the starting point for the passive human being? Here in this place I'm living with that question. If you're able to contribute to the answer, I'll be very grateful.' He was silent for a while and then said: 'I'm already grateful now… for your attention. It's rare.' He smiled. 'How was your journey, Jean? You don't seem at all tired.'

'I like driving. I drive an expensive sports car, speaking of luxury. But I'm not ashamed of it.'

'Why would you be?'

'Because it's 'bad'? I have a great lust for life, I love life. I've enjoyed the trip, the changing countryside, the breaks on the way… so I don't get tired. And I was full of expectation. What I've found here has excelled all my expectations, by the way...'

'I'm very ashamed,' said Jean when they returned to their room to unpack his bag. 'I should've trusted your judgement completely, Maria. All my resistance was based on my fear of losing you... and perhaps even on envy. This man has such *integrity*! More than you and me together... he *consists* of morality, every word, every gesture, his expression, *everything* is steeped with it. And what an inner presence! He calls it inner activity. Well, he is the perfect example of it.'

'What's so good about you, Jean... is that you don't become insecure about it. You remain your quiet, supportive self. You are very 'present' yourself too. The two of you seemed like two good friends meeting again after a long time.'

'It also felt like that for me. I experienced an enormous *power* in the meeting, a potentising of all the good will slumbering inside me. One would want to give all one's effort to this man, to help his endeavours. Enough of all the external nonsense, and only effort for a... so to say, improvement of this sad world in which we live. Inner activity, birth of the new man, new wine in new bottles.'

He looked at her.

She felt his strength, as she had felt it when they first met. Actually, he was all dynamism. But as with all people, his qualities had become bound up in the strain of professional life, in the cares of daily existence. With his dynamism he had built up the law office; he had made it big, but success could not give him the deep satisfaction that man is really looking for. She wrapped her arms around him and pressed him against her.

'Ah, I know you so well!' she sighed.

'You should've forced me, Maria. You shouldn't have waited for ten years!'

'Yes, I should. It's good like this. Only now do I have something to say and a contribution to make here, to Johannes. He already has enough people around him who're dependent. I had to get going by myself.'

'But you did blame me for that, I've felt it.'

'Of course, the longing for Johannes was great. Very. Nevertheless, I couldn't torment you, Jean. It was a torment for you, wasn't it?'

'You're so dear to me, Maria…'

'Look, all human activity is developing in the direction of decadence. The time when man could be truly fertile and create from that, is long gone. Those creative powers that once worked through inspiration have withdrawn in order to give humanity the freedom to know and develop *itself*. If man remains passive and thinks he can create something out of that passivity, the passive void attracts other forces, countervailing forces that are only too happy to speak through him. Humanity's becoming the speaking-tube of these countervailing forces. Oh… what they say is often charming, thrilling, even beautiful. For they're seducers, those counter-forces.'

It was late at night, they were sitting with Johannes and Eva in the living room. Jean had asked what possibilities Johannes saw for modern man to engage in that inner activity after all. Johannes went on:

272

'One possible way is the way of suffering. That will inevitably be poured out on mankind to wake it up – if it doesn't wake up by itself. There's an alternative path before that and it has its point of origin in dissatisfaction of any kind. That's also how it went with us, as we sit here. The flourishing practices of psychotherapists are based on that inner dissatisfaction, on unsatisfied longings.'

'But when one calls for inner activity, there's no one at home?' Jean asked concluding.

Johannes smiled.

'It's like that, but literally. Man is more and more absent in himself, filled with external world-content. How does one speak to somebody who's only half-present?'

'Scream loudly? Grab them by the collar?'

'To catch their attention a little more subtly seems a better way to me. It fits the ideal of freedom more,' Johannes said, smiling.

'But how?'

'To captivate their attention with help of the beauty of abstract, universal thinking is almost impossible. Also in education, even at university, the area of pure, ordinary scientific thinking is giving way to thinking that addresses the reality of practical problems in life, of any kind. We call that problem-directed education.'

'Are you against that?'

'Not directly *against*. I see great benefits in it. But that way, thinking can never develop in a body-free area. The idea of thinking as an individual human source of unity disappears, because it's no longer there, and so can't be experienced.'

'So what then? How do we go on then with the idea of thinking?'

'In the phase of life in which it does *not* have to be there, in the toddler and primary school period, children are pushed into abstraction, and at university, where abstract thinking should be taught in order to awaken body-free thinking, young people are locked in their bodies.'

'So how to proceed then, Johannes?' Jean insisted. 'Your name reminds us of the summons: 'Make straight the way of the Lord!' You are a voice in the wilderness. How can you get through to people with your call?'

'Eventually, Christ had to come to earth to perform a *deed*; the summons of John was only to prepare Christ's path.'

'He's not going to appear in the flesh anymore. But what if He were to return and we didn't *see* Him, because we hadn't washed our eyes?'

'You don't give up, do you? If I truly had the answer, I'd give it to you. I'm living with the question, Jean. The answer lies in self-knowledge. You'll be the first one to hear it from me – if you don't already find it yourself first.'

'To Johannes it must be a great problem that people want to stay passive. He asks me a question in the morning, and in the evening I return it unanswered and give him the task of answering it. And I'm certainly not the only one who treats him like that.'

They were sitting in their bedroom, talking. Maria said:

'It's also hard for him, if not impossible, to answer exactly that question. For to him, it just doesn't apply! His whole

274

being is inner activity, complete presence. How must he imagine that one would not *feel like* that?'

'I don't think that you can imagine that. So it's a fine question for me, because I know that laziness very well, but at least I *realize* that it leads to destruction, to the complete decadence of our human race. What is my motive for inner activity? If I'm completely honest: *you* are, Maria. I'd fall back into complete insecurity if I couldn't join you. I would've gained the insight without you, but I wouldn't have done anything with it. Get it?'

'You could also think: she has a certain talent; let her be.'

'Oh no! It's all too clear to me that talent can be awakened by every human being in himself. I'm just a little too arrogant to stay behind.'

'Still, a lot of people are satisfied with that, even when they meet Johannes. They say: He's just blessed; he has charisma. We'll never achieve that anyway.'

'I'm not like that. He's the great ideal of the Americans, but internally: he's a 'self- made man'. He has 'captured' his inner activity, recreated it. But one can't *be* like that; one can only *become* like it. One must find the courage to remain in continuous *becoming* and not want to rest in *being*. But there's a great gift connected to that. Giving up passivity is rewarded with an everlasting, joyful cheerfulness that is always there – like a kind of continuous bass – around sadness and sorrow. A peaceful, passive *being* only inevitably leads in the end to depression and nervousness, to fundamental insecurity.'

'Can we do something for Johannes? Do you see a possibility?'

Jean nodded cautiously.

'I feel a whole world of possibilities, only I don't have them all clearly before me yet. They'll become clearer this week.'

She couldn't sleep. The meeting between Johannes and Jean had gone so differently from what she had expected. Jean had suddenly become a completely different man whom she had experienced only now and then in their normal life together. Her love was for that being that had now shown itself so completely. It was as if his whole personality, all his experience, his knowledge, his highest virtues assembled in one point in order to appear as a united power in the light of his meeting with Johannes.

One could rightly call such a thing a *miracle*. She felt Jean's morality, his goodness. He had a depth that seemed incomprehensible sometimes; now she saw it deep down...

The question had touched her too. Where *is* the point of application at which the passive man can become active?

The *moment* is very important, the time must be right. If one is called to inner activity too early, the call will be rejected. It has nothing to do with age. At eighty years old one can still be 'too young'. Apparently, one must come to a developmental threshold and it is necessary that one also *experiences* that threshold. That one feels that there is no way out anymore, that there is only that huge abyss in front of you, while behind you there is only the past, of which you are utterly exhausted.

There has to be an understanding in some way or other, an experience of *how* powerless and shadowlike normal consciousness actually is. A longing for reality, for completely saturated content in the consciousness, must awaken, or be awakened. For in our consciousness everything becomes powerless... one can think the most awful thoughts without any disturbance of one's soul. That is the power of the intellect. One can even train oneself in that and then move over from such awful thoughts to acts which do not disturb the conscience. Naturally, there is a different side to man, where that power *does* live. In that place live passion and ardour, but without intellect. All reasoning consideration stops there; one bypasses the abyss of conscience along that other pole. There is a powerful reality, a warmth and a commitment, but they are based on nothing other than the power of temporary selfishness. This gets its powers from the mortal body and everything that connected to it: blood, homeland, race, religious fanaticism... The true man lives neither in the one nor in the other pole... but in the balance between the two. Schiller already wrote about this in his letters on the aesthetic education of man. Goethe depicted the process in his wonderful 'Fairy Tale of the Green Snake and the Beautiful Lily'.

Man today is in danger of losing himself in these two opposites, but is able to feel over and over again the summons to approach the threshold and come to an aware, conscientious power.

Threshold experiences are necessary to be able to hear the summons that will always come to you at such times - from an event, a book, a meeting... And hearing alone is not enough, one must *listen actively*, one must do something. Starting to strive and never stop, wanting to become that human being who is master of both poles, who can use them for the honour and glory of mankind.

Maria sighed and fell asleep.

*

Agnes thought that she could go back to work again. The examination had only showed two slight narrowings; the rest was spasms of the coronary vessels and could be handled with medication. She had to watch out a little for stress, but beyond that, it was only a storm in a teacup.

That is how she described it at the dinner table. The children looked at her with big eyes. René did not look at her at all; it was as if he was not listening. She shrugged and said:

'You're looking at me as if you're seeing a monster,' and helped herself to another serving. But after dinner, René said:

'Come with me to my study for a minute, Agnes.'

She followed him while the children cleared the table. He sat down. He was the psychiatrist; she was the patient.

'Yes, doctor?' she asked mockingly, but René was undisturbed. He looked straight at her and said:

'You're not quite normal, Agnes.'

'Then I'm in the right place here.'

'Stop it! With those slight narrowings and those spasms you nevertheless did have a stroke, didn't you? Without even noticing.'

278

'That happens often. I'm on medication now. That'll prevent it.'

'What confidence! Where are you, Agnes? You were just coming out, you were coming to yourself, to a certain earnestness. Now it's all better than expected and instead of transforming your gratitude into deep contemplation, you're starting to run again. Until you'll collapse completely.'

'I'm not made for profundity. I want to *do* something.'

'I know, I know you. But this time I won't allow it. If you had a different job... all right. But your part-time job is forty, fifty hours a week. We love you, Agnes, me... and the children.'

She felt that she was blushing. Who could love her! René reached out to her and took her hand in his two wise hands. She looked at them and said shyly:

'What am I doing here, René? So many hours a day. Longing for you to come home, to sit here with you. I read a fairy-tale every day and form images; they become clearer and clearer, richer, more real. But what do I have to do with them? They call up strong mood-movements which I don't know what to do with. I'm always longing... for you, for Maria, for daddy and mommy... for Johannes... for the children. And when you are here, I don't know how to handle it. I fall back into my old way of behaving. Beautiful, harsh Agnes...'

'That's understandable... you can't turn your whole habit-life around at once, nobody's asking that from you.'

'It bothers me. I feel like I'm in two pieces, do you understand?'

'So you opt entirely for the beautiful, harsh Agnes?'

She collapsed inwardly and sighed.

'I know that's no longer possible. The real Agnes has come out too much to be able to keep ignoring her. But it's a kind of condemnation to something that's very hard to accept.'

'And Johannes?'

'What do you mean?'

'Have you spoken to him lately?'

'No. I can't come to him with my plan to go to work again. He makes it clear to me that he's fed up with having to pull people. I have to decide myself: or I'll start working on myself, or not. If the latter, then I don't have to see him anymore. As an old friend I can, but not for advice... But René, I can't put all my abilities into my own development, surely? That can't be right either?'

'You're sick, Agnes.... in which case, it is very right.'

'I am not sick. Since I've been taking those pills, I feel nothing anymore.'

'Quit taking them and you'll soon notice.'

She sighed again.

'What do I have to do, then?'

'First go to Johannes in the summer and see what you can do. I'll come with the children for a couple of weeks and stay in the neighbourhood in a hotel. After that, we'll see."

She walked into the city and now she stood in the Bonneterie with a pile of discounted shirts. Light blue would look good under his blue blazer; it made him more masculine... but such squares looked good beneath a woollen sweater.

She liked to dress René to her taste. And well-behaved, he put on what she bought for him.

'It's not easy to make a choice when there's so much to choose from,' an unknown male voice said next to her. She looked into the blue eyes of a tall, greying man. He was wearing an expensive camel coat. She noticed a gold watch… and a handsome head. A Dracula-head, or a vampire…? Such a noble face, but when he pursed his lips in a smirk, he showed his true nature. The man smiled broadly in answer to her thoughts – the only thing she saw was a golden crown in the back of his mouth. Why wasn't she more like Maria? *She* would walk away immediately, perhaps after a friendly nod of her head. Chapter closed. No, Agnes enjoyed the feeling that she was still an attractive woman at fifty years of age. She smiled back at him, took the light blue shirt off the pile and said:

'I'll take this one. You should always imagine what it'll look like; that makes it very easy to choose.'

'Advise me then, will you? What should I wear with this jacket?'

Now she would usually answer: call the saleswoman, I'll pay for this. But instead, she looked at his checked jacket and said:

'White. Something white would go well with that, like this one.'

Together they walked to the cash desk, where they had to wait a little while.

'Will you have a cup of coffee with me, here in Corona?' he asked.

She nodded and a little later, they walked, both with a

carrier bag, along the street towards Corona. She hadn't done this for a long time, going with a good-looking man just like that. Perhaps that was why she had those heart cramps, from all that suppressing what she actually liked. They sat opposite each other, at a table by the window.

'Do you live in The Hague?' she asked.

'No, in Utrecht. I had a business meeting here. And you?'

'Yes, I do. It's a boring city, but Utrecht is not much better. I prefer Amsterdam; I studied there.'

She wanted him to ask her: What did you study? He asked:

'What is your profession?'

'I'm a surgeon.'

That had the expected effect. She changed into Dracula herself, a frightening person with a knife and scissors… she looked into his blue eyes and suddenly she realized that she felt sick. Imagine going on with this and going with him to a hotel room – like she used to do. Had she never felt how *foreign* such a body is? She thought of René, with whom she was thoroughly familiar, with whom she had four children. *Four* children! So much common experiences in misery and happiness…. And this man across the table… an attractive man, she could sleep with him, she felt that only too well. She could be grateful to this man. He had made her realise that all this was far, far behind her. Suppressing what she liked? She did not like it anymore; she got a lot more feeling now from the reality of her life. As a girl she had lived outside reality… dragged along by her coquettishness… a thin line of unreality. She did not have to please René anymore; he had stayed with her for thirty years through thick and thin. And this light blue shirt would suit him well… she drank her coffee, got up and said:

'Thanks for the cosy chat.'

She shook his hand and left him bewildered.

She was *so* happy, she could have skipped like a child. Her joy was too great for her to walk like a lady… The image of the man came back to her. He had been a test. 'Life is a fairy-tale', she sang silently on the inside… nothing is boring, each step is development. I'd thought that I couldn't come any further, that I would remain the bad old Agnes forever – and I didn't know how life has shaped me. Life, people. She could embrace everyone! The Hofvijver lake and the buildings of the Binnenhof looked like a fairy-tale… The Hague a boring city? Not at all… happiness is everywhere, if only you have it with you. At home she found her eldest son in front of the TV… Why did she suddenly see him sitting there? He sat there a lot, every day. Now a certain despondency struck her.

'What's wrong, Paul?'

He shrugged his shoulders bluntly. A sixteen year-old does not talk to the enemy, his mother, just like that.

'Would you like something to eat? Shall I make you something?'

The boy looked up, surprised.

'Something good? Do you have something good?'

'A sandwich, a sandwich with fried egg, tea with cookies? Name it.'

He got up and turned off the TV.

'I have a maths test tomorrow and I don't get it at all. Nobody can help me; they can't explain anything to me. I'd like a sandwich.'

He walked with her to the kitchen, a big boy, a child.

'Go and get your book. We can look at it together.'

'As if you'd understand it,' he grumbled.

'You'll be surprised,' she grinned.

She sang to herself as she made his sandwich,

A life of haste and waiting… the expectation of compliments from the outside world. Everything, everything was led by the outside world, only her coquettishness and haste came from inside. Fear too… mostly fear, that's where the haste came from. Fifty years on the run… well, forty, forty-five years. A young child does not live like that yet; everything just simply goes by. However, she had certainly been a difficult and naughty child, a challenge for her parents, a challenge for Maria.

Maria… how she sometimes longed for her! She had hated and appreciated her, loved her and loathed her. Now she was longing for her, although she blamed her for going to Johannes with Jean just like that. For Johannes was *her* friend. René had always adored Maria; that had never changed – and now she had had to experience that Johannes chose her above his old, faithful, but spirit-despising friend Agnes.

Why did she long for Maria? She had a silence about her, a calm, a quiet, rest. She must be a fine mother, a fine wife too. She was never on the go; she was always just there, in all the open attention that one could expect from a human being. Coquettishness? Maria did not need that because she evoked sympathy without doing anything for it. Probably she had such great self-confidence because of her calmness – or calmness because of her self-confidence? Oh… Agnes had basically always looked up to her, even as a child already. But *she* was more energetic, prettier… and with those qualities, she had raised herself high above Maria; she had chosen *Maria's* boyfriend as her husband, and with those same qualities, she had made herself a career…. Outwardly, Maria did not seem to amount to anything much. Still she longed for her, as one can long for one's parents, for ones childhood. It would be obvious to grab the phone and call her up – or even take the train to Maastricht; she had plenty of time. But she could not do it; it was impossible for her. She could not approach her and she did not know exactly why….

'What actually is your feeling for Maria, René? You used to be in love with her, you stayed in contact with her even though she rejected you. What did you see in her, what do you still see in her?'

'Are you jealous?'

'No! It's just a question, I have a lot of time to ask myself all kinds of questions.'

René thought about it for a while.

'Well,' he said. 'How should one express someone's being, other than naming the name? Maria. She is the finest woman I've ever met. I saw that then and I see it now; she remains absolutely at the top. She is… unencumbered, free, pure, honest. She used to be very melancholic. I also thought that was very beautiful. Now that her longing is satisfied, she has found her spiritual home. She's not robust, but fragile... and yet durable. Like the blossom of her beloved apple-tree, with the firm will to bear fruit. And above all, she's very sweet, kind. Her presence gives comfort and hope. That's about it.'

'But she has no... she's not a woman of passion.'

René smiled at her.

'You are comparing her to yourself. There is little similarity.'

'Why, for God's sake, did you start a relationship with me?'

'Because *you* are Agnes. You are tops in a different way. Maria was out of my league, too high up there for a whiner like me.'

'So you settled for the bad sister.'

'I fell in love with you at first sight. The two loves I felt were as much alike as the two sisters.'

'In love? With me?'

'What else did you think?'

She sighed very deeply.

'You could've said that, René! I've always felt like a surrogate for her.'

She felt her loneliness, a bottomless self-pity.

René felt it too and jumped up to embrace her.

'We've made it right, Agnes! We've found each other, we talk a lot, we're happy to be together. We have beautiful children.'

'I'm so alone. I always *have* been. What's the sense of all this?'

286

'Development, it seems. Growth.'

'In order to discover that I'm the weakest of all?'

'Come on, Agnes! You're brave, active, pretty, intelligent. What do you mean *weak*!?'

'I can't find myself anymore. Who is Agnes? A shadow.'

'A shadow is always cast by 'something' on which the light falls.'

'Then let me find that 'something!'

He held her close. It helped; she felt something of herself in his power.

'Do you see something in me besides external beauty and so on?' she asked softly.

'You move me. Now all the fuss is falling away…'

'Is there something left of me then, René?'

'You are more than you ever were, love. More than ever.'

She sat in the garden in the sun. René was at work, the children at school. Inside the house, music was playing, a oboe concerto by Bach. Music touched her more and more, a life with René was a life with music. Who is Agnes…? A yearning being, full of longing for love. And what about the hate? She could hate very powerfully, hate ugliness, weakness, laziness. But that was a hollow shadow, that being that was *not*; it was filled with negativity, because it had an affinity with negativity. Is it possible to step into true *being* from the shadow? From void to fullness, from hate to love? Can one decide on that and do it? Abruptly end one's old existence and start a new life, like Francis of Assisi? Or must it be done gradually, in a continuous metamorphosis? A human being is capable of a lot, but the *will* is lacking. Ordinary life is a façade. Maria had always felt that. It was what made her so different from the others. Could one be the twin sister of such a person and remain completely untouched by that? Apparently not … the longing for her sister grew constantly. *Maria* was the true successor of daddy. She had not talked

to daddy; she and he had only spoken when necessary. That could not happen a second time; she wanted to try to really get to know her sister....

Of plunderers I am death, the vanquisher of all recollection; and of the predestined six transformations of the living beings I am birth, the foremost. Of ladies, I am the seven qualities of a good wife grace, beauty, perfect speech, remembrance, intelligence, patience, and forgiveness.

Bhagavad Gita, 10 vers 34.

What are *you* doing here!?' Agnes stood in front of Maria, her eyes glittering brightly. They had met each other unexpectedly, in the park at the institute in the mountains. Both were visiting Johannes. She looked stunning, dressed in an expensive summer dress, her shoulders naked, her black hair perfectly dressed. She had an admirable physical energy, a blinding beauty. Maria no longer felt insecure in her presence, even though it was overwhelming. She remained calm and answered:

'Jean and I are staying with Johannes. He's invited us to spend our summer holiday here.'

Agnes paused, bewildered. Staying with Johannes? She was staying in one of the rooms in the main building, like one of the many students and visitors, yes, even as a patient....

Maria felt sorry for her. She said:

'It's typical of our relationship that we haven't heard this from each other, isn't it,? Shall we have a drink together, Agnes?'

Agnes pretended to be indifferent, while inside, she was full of longing.

'All right,' she said with a shrug.

'Where's René?' Maria asked. 'And the children?'

289

'Still at home, but they're coming next week. They've been able to rent a house in the neighbourhood.'

'What're you doing here, Agnes? I mean… what're you occupied with?'

They walked in the direction of the main building.

'Learning to be humble,' mocked Agnes. 'Twice a week I have a conversation with that creep, the master. Obligatory. He gives me a metaphorical beating; my whole being is bare to him.'

'Obligatory? You certainly don't have to?'

'Yes… it's one of the conditions that Johannes has laid down for my stay here. I'm getting to know him very differently now. He used to be a friendly, kind brother to me. Now he is very strict….'

'You must want it yourself, then. Johannes always leaves everyone free.'

'Of course I want it myself – and at the same time *not at all*.'

They sat across from each other at a table in the dining room. Agnes' attitude softened a little.

'I've been wanting to meet you very much, Maria. I'm sorry for my unfriendliness… of course, I didn't expect you to be here. We never see each other and we rarely speak. I regret that.'

She bowed her head so that she did not have to see Maria's reaction.

'I always feel connected to you, Agnes, no matter what. Don't you feel that?'

When Agnes looked up, her eyes were big and wet.

'I do… as longing. I would love to be your friend, talk to

you like you did with daddy. I am *so* lonely, Maria.'

Maria put a hand on Agnes's and squeezed it.

'Did you think that I don't have that longing? You're inaccessible, Agnes, I can't reach you. We speak a different language.'

'Not anymore… I'm not so bad anymore. I've been through a lot. With René, with the children, in my profession, with my illness. I'm not so silly anymore.'

'I never thought you were… you were only inaccessible.'

She looked at Agnes. She looked very different now, like she had peeled off a skin. She had always been straight and inaccessible, proud and rejecting. Now she seemed to be dynamic and open, but mostly very sad.

'I'm starting to experience myself and I can talk to no-one. René loves me too much; he doesn't want to hear anything about my weaknesses – and Johannes is *so* severe! He thinks that feelings of guilt are egoistic and passive. An excuse not to start working. That's true… but they don't see how hard it is. Well, they *do* see that… but they don't want to comfort me. Daddy would have understood; I am sure about that. And you, Maria… you must understand too.'

'Johannes understands it, for sure, Agnes… and I do too.'

A tear rolled down Agnes' beautiful cheek. She wiped it and said softly:

'Of course he understands. He's a great man, really. He must treat me like this, or else I'd go and sit in the sun all day… but I'm so lonely, Maria.'

Maria nodded while she held her sister's hand.

She felt her despair, how all the old seemed to have left her, but there was nothing new yet to draw from.

291

'Tell me, Agnes? What do you have to do here?'

'Those two times a week I go to the master. To his house, in his meditation room. I'm afraid of that, those carpets on the floor and the tapestries on the walls, and then such a simple bare chair which I have to sit on, and then his eyes that see through me like X-rays. I feel what *he* sees, do you understand? And it's nothing good. My fear, my hate, my scepticism, my cynicism… but also my nerve, my success… I feel how much luck I have had, actually in everything.'

'You have your talents to thank for that!'

'Yes, but those are founded on self-assertion. He sees that, and I feel it. In the meantime, he says all kind of things, he tries to teach me how to look without judgement. For example, he asked me why his meditation room scares me so much. The atmosphere there is ancient, but also threatening, as if an elephant could come in the room at any moment that would blast me away with its trunk, or a wild tiger that would eat me. The master roars with laughter then, but he does think that what I become aware of is correct, only it is reinforced, exaggerated by my fear. I have to train myself in artistic observation, but then try to obtain a more objective point of view, try not to add personal feelings to it. He likes me, he appreciates that elemental emotional life – but it has to be transformed.'

'And Johannes? Does he give you assignments?'

'He's a doctor and a teacher at the same time. Of course, I've actually come here to be freed from my physical problems. But according to him, those come from my compulsive way of being – so that is what must be worked on.

The physical body is comforted by warmth, fragrant leaves and massages. But the soul gets copped, also by him – although he is also kind, of course.'

' How?'

'He's to blame for the fact that I *feel* myself so strongly. I've been reading fairy-tales and thinking them through in images. That calls for enormous self-knowledge... in visual feelings – it's a *hell*. René keeps telling me to read Dante, but that's too complicated for me.'

'And what else?'

'I talk to him three times a week. It's strange when a man who's an old good friend suddenly detaches himself from you and becomes your teacher. I've never known him like that before; we were always in tune with each other.'

'Why shouldn't a teacher be in tune with you?'

Agnes looked at her, hesitating. Maria was touched by her physical beauty, which suddenly had such a *softness*.

'Could that be? I don't experience it like that, in any case. I'm still seeking his friendship. There's nobody in my life who has given me *so* much friendship as he has. But now he sets conditions – otherwise, my stay here doesn't make any sense, I do understand that. I mainly train myself in *contemplation*. Looking back on what I actually experience over and over again - that's the main assignment. I've always lived on the outside; I've always *presented* myself strongly. Now that power has to turn around a little. When I reflect, morality and conscience start to speak up in me. That's not easy, Maria. When daddy died, Johannes had already summoned me above all to *experience* profoundly what I felt. I didn't want to respond to that; I put away my

293

grief, it was *too* hard for me. Now, because of my heart condition, I have to contemplate. Of course, I could leave it to
the pills I take, I also believe in that. But daddy was also *my*
father, Johannes is also *my* friend, you're also *my* sister…
you've also left something inside me, a vague trust in God,
a doubt in materialism. I really wanted to ask daddy: what
do you think of me – and who *are* you actually? Now, I'm
at the point where I could ask him that question but at that
time it was impossible. I see him sitting there, on a worn-
out chair in the sun in front of the kitchen window, his
eyes closed, perhaps in deep prayer. When I think of that,
Maria, I have to cry and can't stop crying. What a blessing
to have had such a father – what negligence to have lived
my life past him, ignoring him like that, *so* negligent. Then
I think: imagine that God does exist, that He really had
his Son come to be with us until the end of the world. The
negligence with which I live past *that* fact is a negligence
that's unfathomable – if it were true.'

'Is it true, Agnes?'

'How should I know? I've never believed it. It was easier
not to.'

'Is it true?'

Agnes took her head into her hands.

'Yes, of course it's true,' she said softly. 'Everybody knows
it. *Everybody*. We only don't want it to be true, it's too trou-
blesome. In Germany, I came across a booklet: "Good girls
go to heaven, bad girls get what they want." Those girls are
you and me, Maria.'

'I also get what I want, Agnes.'

'More than I do, probably. Only the others don't realise it;

294

that's hard for a woman like me. I want to be *seen*.... You're sweet, Maria. A sweet sister you are. I feel too weak to carry all that grief. So much regret... yearning... longing...'

The beautiful brown eyes filled with tears and one rolled down her cheek. Maria took her hand firmly again and said:

'Don't look back too much, Agnes... it paralyzes you. You should look ahead. We can still experience so many good things.'

'I *must* look back. That's where the power of contemplation is. There's no getting away from that, Maria. I shall have to learn to endure the love I feel... for you, from you.'

'How can it be that you've changed *so* much, Agnes? Is it only because of the heart problems?'

Agnes shook her head and blew her nose.

'No, those are side-issues; they've only been a reason for me to consult Johannes. He brought a change to my life already once before.... I wasn't able to combine his friendship with my unfaithfulness to René. I couldn't look into Johannes' eyes and cheat on my husband at the same time. That's just not possible. That was contemplation already, but very weak, faint, more in passing. Now that I've visited him here, I am kind of desperate. It's his being that's changing me, although he doesn't intervene at all; he's just who he is. That's great, the way he is. I would've loved to have him as my husband... but of course, I see how impossible that was. With him I would've drowned in self-reproach. It's his love... or mine for him that's making me change. He's just a man, if a *man* can have such an effect, how must one ever face Our Good Lord – *if* he exists?'

295

'Does He exist, Agnes?' Maria asked again. She felt how strongly Agnes felt His reality – and yet still doubted it.

Agnes sighed deeply.

'Terrible, isn't it? Always doubting what I'm sure of. I'm bound to become a wreck like this. But I think that what I'm going through now, experiencing... that He is that. Johannes lives in following Him. It's not Johannes, but it's His example, something like that... Daddy was an example, *you* are... but he is *so* strongly, at least for me there is no escaping from it anymore.'

'Do you still want to escape?'

No... but life was so easy, it went so well... but it was *empty*. Now it's brimming, but the fullness hurts.'

Agnes looked at Maria silently for a while. Maria... *so* familiar and still *so* foreign. She asked:

'And you, Maria, what're you doing here exactly?'

Maria nodded pensively and answered:

'We were here for two weeks last spring. Johannes and I talked a lot. He guided me at the time, after daddy's funeral – and I never spoke to him again after that. It was about time now. What I didn't expect, was that Jean and he would immediately become the best of friends. They went for a walk together, Jean fixed some legal jobs... and of course we loved to come back this summer. Jean is busy modernising the administration; I only see him in the evenings and on Sundays. In the meantime, I try to find the connection between... what I experience as powers in thinking and observation – and the creating powers of nature, especially in my own nature, the body. I do the rounds with Eva, she is completely comfortable in that area, she truly lives there. For me, those rounds are real revelations, insight into a completely new medicine, which doesn't reject the old school medicine, but complements it completely – only it doesn't stop there, but develops *further*, on and on. Perhaps there's a task for me there in the future, I'm not sure yet.'

Maria saw from Agnes eyes that she had dropped out and could not follow her anymore. But she did not mock, she said:

'I don't get it at all, although you're obviously speaking Dutch! Johannes is my doctor; I rarely see Eva. I'm very jealous of her, although I accept the situation the way it is, of course. She *has* what we all want: she's married to the king.'

Maria burst out laughing.

'Are you really so dissatisfied with your life? With René... and the children?'

'No. I'm beginning to understand that what makes Johannes so special lives in all of us – even in me. He has something in him that's universal and still completely individual. I would love to lean against it, for protection... but I must do it myself! You know, it is like I've been lounging in the sun like a kitten on the windowsill all my whole life. And now...I suddenly realize that I'm a *human being*, who's born to *develop* herself, instead of just lounging. René's had his nose in his books for thirty years; he *knows* so incredibly much. He has really become a wise man because of that; I admire that in him. He isn't such an abstract thinker, he *experiences* what he reads, and through that he develops in his own way, even if it's more horizontally; he doesn't really

297

rise like you and Johannes. I do *see* all that, Maria.'

Maria was still smiling. She said:

'I never thought of you as a kitten! More like a panther, or a tiger. Someone to reckon with!'

Now Agnes smiled too.

'I've been longing for an animal trainer. Someone who can crack a whip over me,' she sighed. 'But I have to deal with it myself. The sun shines on all of us, but not *inside* all of us. One seems to have to do something about that oneself.' She stretched her beautiful body and said: 'Come on, I have a meeting with Johannes. I can't be late. When shall we talk again, sister?'

They made a date for lunch, and Agnes walked through the hall to Johannes room. She had tears in her heart, but also gratitude. It is painful to let love in, but at the same time, it gives value to life...

She knocked on the door. It door swung open and Johannes stood before her. 'What makes Johannes so special lives in each person, even in me.' she repeated to herself. She shook his hand and sat down. Without waiting, she asked:

'How did you come this far, Johannes? What've you done to awaken the sun inside yourself? When you were young, you already had that... but it was very fragile and light. You've gone through an enormous development, Johannes. If only we let inside what we observe, we see a lot... I've noticed little in my life; I lived past your quality without noticing it – although I've pleasantly taken advantage of it.'

Johannes seemed to shine more than ever; apparently one sees what one can endure. He said:

'Our bodies would fade too early and become wooden if

life inside us wasn't fructified with the power of resurrection – even when one doesn't believe in it. There's an inner path that leads to contact with that power of resurrection. We can become aware that it's there, live in it, learn to observe in it. One begins that path as a philosopher – *not* how philosophy is normally studied – but as a human being who wants to research that, who wants to know what it is, who wants to make it into experience, instead of only using it in *knowing*. The scientific experience of knowing – of human intelligence – is the first phase of *spiritual science*. That knowing deepens, and broadens, but mostly becomes *stronger*. You can follow it into areas where you would *never* come with ordinary, contemplative thinking, areas where the power of thinking is a power of physical growth. Then the philosopher becomes a biologist and ultimately, a doctor. But these skills shouldn't be understood in the way we teach them at university. One's no longer facing life with one's intelligence, facing the body, but one lives, experiencing, *in* it. One knows it from the *inside out*, without a distance between the observer and the observed, thus without any doubts, but still in complete objectivity.'

'Maria said about the same thing this morning. But that doesn't explain your radiation to me, Johannes. That you're wise, and have knowledge and clairvoyance, I believe it straightaway. But that's not what I mean....'

The man facing her, whom she knew as if he was her big brother, smiled. She felt his smile like a wistful touch on her painful heart. It was as though his smile was a living substance, something curative. He said:

'You've changed, Agnes!'

299

'I'm only living a little bit more inwardly than I used to. I feel more, I am more calm. Otherwise, I'm still exactly the same, beautiful on the outside, and on the inside…. well.'

'The outside is also a result of the inside, even though there's still a great abyss between hereditary talent and individuality. True beauty points to bridging that abyss.'

'But you've avoided my question – and I'm really asking that question in all earnestness now. I was raised a Catholic; my father was a truly religious man. I really know that from my experience in childhood. How did you get the sun inside you, Johannes, which makes you a blessing all around you ?'

He shook his head.

'It really went the way I described just now. The path is a widening of knowledge. But just that widening, that *spreading power…* is the sun. The more one may enlarge one's knowledge, the more intensely that inner power starts to enlighten and warm. Don't think that everyone in my environment observes what you mean. You must have a link to it, or else you don't recognise that inner sun eludes you completely, not in the other *and* not in yourself.'

'My father also had that inner radiation, although he never worked on widening of his inner knowledge.'

'That's grace, Agnes. St. Paul didn't work on his inner knowledge either when he observed the risen Christ on the road to Damascus. Through grace He exposes Himself to whomever He wants. But besides that, every human being has received the freedom to seek Him *consciously* and know Him. Those people *must* be there, for He *wants* to be known in freedom. They find Him in the power that widens knowledge. He *is* that power, and as a human being, one only has to want it *oneself.* There's not only a fulfilment of the spirit, a blessing... but also a complete awareness of it, not only *that* He is present, but also *who* He is and how He can be found. In Him gradually the whole spiritual world comes to appearance, which is, of course, no less complicated and rich in beings than the earth is. There is no undefined All filled with bliss. The spiritual world comprises also the spiritual part of the earth; it goes into the deepest matter and shapes it. So the deepening of our medical knowledge is without end, you surely see that?'

This had made her dizzy; she was feeling really dizzy. One did not *want* to believe such a thing, for many, many reasons. For a man who wants to remain with the ordinary sensory consciousness is *tiny.* Tiny and weak. Who wants to be like that? But wanting to develop one's knowledge takes one immediately into a realm of infinite powerlessness, because one is not at all able to achieve it! She could see a human being in her sister, who had walked very far along that path – and in Johannes a human being who probably was even a lot further along the path. *So* far that was he almost out of sight. But no, he was sitting there opposite her. A man of flesh and blood, but also of soul and spirit. She shivered.

'Is there something that I can do?' she asked insecurely. It was as if her whole being, her life, her ambition, her passion, her battle with René, her worries about her children, the grief about daddy, about Maria... loosened from her

301

and were outside her like an image, a remembrance. The importance of it became relative ... why did she worry unnecessarily about side-issues! The question she was asking did not come from that image, but from the being in herself that lived outside that image. She felt alienated from her life, but the alienation did not frighten her; it relieved her.

'This is who you really are,' sounded Johannes voice. 'Beyond time and space, this is who you are.'

She felt how she dove into the image again. Her life was around her again like a glove. Now she asked Johannes from that ordinary image of her life:

'Is there something that I can do, Johannes? Can such an incredibly selfish being like Agnes do anything at all?'

'You've just experienced your *will*, Agnes. That will has worked in every detail of your life to bring you to the threshold where you are now. When you look back, you just see the road back. When you look forward, the abyss of powerlessness is gaping there before you. Whatever development you strive for, everything will take you to the road back. Only willingness to fully experience powerlessness and work on your weak powers of thinking, feeling and willing makes a road forward possible. Your whole life, everything that you have experienced, must be sacrificed at the edge of the abyss, so that it can become a firm bridge to the other side, which is now still invisible. The road back won't give you any satisfaction anymore; the road forward is not yet possible. You're too strong to go back and too weak to go forward. So stop, Agnes, and contemplate. Become strong in yourself by honest observation.'

Agnes walked outside. She had to get some fresh air. Well, fresh… it was hot, too hot. Thunder came on, clouds gathered above her head. In spite of the heat, she shivered. An unpleasant man, Johannes, with his moralising. 'There's no road back, only one forward, but *you* are too stupid and weak for it.'

What did *he* know? He sat there with his handsome head, looking holy, being the great initiate. Initiated in nothing, that's what he was!'

The wind started to blow, it pulled on her beautiful dress, she had to hold it in place with her hands. She was ferocious! She wanted to put her nails in his flesh, teach him to shut his *mouth*! She would just go home, away from this couple of fools, who fancy themselves to be at the top of the world. The fool had let his career go for a delusion! Oh, she was fed up with it! And Maria? Maria….

She loved Maria, more than she wanted to admit. She shivered again and looked around her. She sat down on a bench. The wind died down – nowhere a cloud to be seen. The sky was deep blue, the sun shone brightly on her bronzed skin. Had there been thunder coming on?

Maria… she wanted to go and see her, she felt like crying like a child. Maria, where would she be?

René, she loved René too, she longed for his arrival. René and his books… he was married to his books more than to her.

She sighed.

Johannes. Wasn't that him walking over there, in the distance? The reality of a human being is very different from what one is left with as an image after a meeting. The image consists for the most part from feeling; there is not a lot objective in it, at least, not like the memories *she* cherished.

Now she saw him walking there, he approached her. He was alone, perhaps on his way to the house of his friend, the master. She had just hated him, for everything that he stood for... now she saw his reality, just because he did not see her. She observed a certain loneliness, but also a great *fullness*. He was surrounded by something... just that something she had hated with a power that now worried her. In a little while, he would see her. Then he *did* see her and approached her immediately. He stood before her, while she stayed seated.

'Are you okay?' he asked. Naturally, he saw how she had judged him. She looked him right in the eyes and answered:

'No, Johannes. I'm not okay at all. I'm completely fed up.'

He reached out his hand; she took it and stood up. She felt his warm, firm hand and started to cry very loud. She stamped her feet.

'I'm sorry! I really don't know what to do.'

'Come on, let's take a walk in the direction of the mountains. Speak your mind, Agnes.' He gave her a clean handkerchief, which he apparently always had at hand for crying women.... The gesture made her lose all her self-control. She blew her nose to hide her sobbing.

'I don't know what to do anymore. Everything is upside down – and I blame you for it – and that's not right, of course. I felt this grief once before, when daddy died. It's unbearable, Johannes! You don't know such despair – or do you?'

He took her by the arm to support her.

'Of course I do… I know the feelings of negligence, of farewell, of loneliness… oh, I know them so well.'

'But you are strong, you turn them into power. I drown in them, it's a waterfall… and I drag you along in my fall.'

He pinched her arm and smiled.

'That won't be so easy, you know. Let's say: I'll catch you down there, so you can sail on safely.'

She sighed trembling.

'If I only knew how to go on. I don't want to go on anymore, I'm depressed.'

She felt his compassion, but also his right judgement. He said:

'You're not depressed at all, Agnes. You're just saying something. Yes, you're apparently at a dead end. Stay put now for a while and experience yourself. You'll notice that you're *alive*, Agnes!'

She felt that storm rising again, the wind of hatred. She said:

'You don't know how *empty* I am, Johannes.'

She started crying again. He put his hand on her shoulder.

'Enter into what is there, Agnes. You *feel* empty, but you're not. You've always lived with enthusiasm. Hold on to that, it's your strength.'

'Enthusiasm for myself, yes. Now that self is empty and there's nothing to be happy about.'

'Stop talking nonsense!'

'Then I can only be silent.'

He stood still and took both her shoulders. Her father had never been so strict; he had always understood everything. This man simply did not *want* to understand certain things, because understanding would keep her from development. Still, she was mad at him – and sad to death. First she looked at him, but she could not stand that after all. Not because she thought that she was less than he was, but because she saw that he actually expected something of her, while still leaving her free. Suddenly, she understood his expectation and she said, stammeringly:

'You mean, that my external life is exhausted, don't you? I've got out of it what was in there, everything has played itself out... perhaps it'd already been exhausted for a long time. I can let myself go, and sink into depression – or I can start with a look inside, find that there isn't much there, and start by giving my life *content* consciously. Read René's books, your books, follow your leads to meditation... fight this immensely strong self-interest, the feelings of hate, the fear... or perhaps just give up all the fighting and just go to work. If that's the meaning of it all, why does *everything* inside me revolt? *Everything*!'

'Just stand still, Agnes, and experience what is there. Your powerlessness, your hate. There's only one cure: peaceful observation, honesty, contemplation. That makes every storm pass, it really does. You're intelligent, you're a good observer. Let it be how it is and on the other hand bring yourself to it to utilize your intelligence for something new. Is there nothing in René's library that has your interest?'

'Yes, but I don't like to read and I can't concentrate.'

'How have you studied, then?'

'Through the power of ambition.'

'Can't you reshape that ambition, then?'

'Can I? Am I allowed to strive to become *the best* in spiritual sense?'

Johannes burst out in a liberating laugh.

'Of course you can! Ambition is so right in that area! In striving to perfect oneself, one can want to be the best. It's actually one's only strength. In you, in me, in everyone.'

'So we're a bunch of terrible egoists!'

'You can keep that justified egoism in balance by letting go of it in your daily life. The more you can let things speak for themselves, the greater becomes your strength to be the best in striving towards the spirit.'

Agnes looked up, right in Johannes eyes. She nodded thoughtfully.

'Right,' she said. 'I think I can work with that, if I'm allowed to strive to be the best in one area or the other. I'd thought that it was *bad*, such a target.' She smoothed her skirt and said:

'Come on, Johannes. Why're we still standing here? I want to get to work. Which book should I start with?'

'Start with the first book by the Master of the West, the introductions to Goethe's natural scientific work. When your concentration weakens, think about ambition. With a wink, he shook her hand, turned around and walked off in the direction of the master's house.

She felt something like happiness inside. She was a student again, on the doorstep of a great career and anxious to begin. She would pull together all her energies to start on this study; she was going to show once more who *Agnes* actually is. The only condition was: let go of all ambition, dramatic selfishness and criticism in daily life. That was naturally a giant condition, but she felt that she had it in her. She had a strength with which one can achieve anything, if one only really wanted to. And *wanting* – she knew something about that. If René had not have constrained her, she would certainly have become a professor. Now she would apply that strength internally; she would do everything a student in spiritual science has to do – and she would give up *all* external glory, however hard it was bound to be for her. Only Johannes would know about her progress, perhaps Maria a little bit too. The sun high up there could rise within her after all, for she already *felt* it now, just by the very intention!

The fairy-tale of the soot-black brother of the devil had worked in her; she suddenly saw now that the will can be applied for evil, or for good; it is the same will. The choice is free, in both cases one must at first be the king of oneself. She too was released from the duty of life and had walked in the forest, sad and despondent. Yet Johannes had appeared to her instead of the devil… and she knew now what to do. Long years of service to the spirit were in front of her and the only thing that she had in her was ambition. With that she would wash herself clean and she would succeed…. Energetic and self-aware, she walked to the main building, where she would have dinner with Maria.

Maria saw her sister entering the room. A fifty year-old woman, approaching her like a girl. She was always a radiant beauty, next to whom she soon felt like an uninteresting, grey mouse. Her sister's beauty had always been something surprising, even a bit aggressive. One felt the beauty of the forest, where one always had to be careful.

She was more ordinary now, less impressive. Actually, they looked like each other, she and Agnes. She had not retouched her make-up, her hair was a little bit messy and her smile had something shy about it. She hugged Maria and kissed her three times. She sat down and said:

'I'm so happy, Maria. I can't say *how* happy I am! It'll all be different now, you'll see!'

'What's happened to you in the last couple of hours?'

'I've suddenly understood something. The most beautiful thing in life is to be on the path, isn't it? That's why I loved college so much. My whole life was in front of me and I was going to make it! Now we are 'arrivées', and there's nothing left to achieve. I was plodding along on my way to nowhere. The endpoint of the road was already visible, death was grinning up ahead, waiting for the prey that I had prepared myself. Everything precious in life has to be given to him. Your money, your possessions – your body. He's already taking pieces away from you now, by aging you… you become ugly, wrinkly, shrivelled. You put a layer of make-up on and it's all right again. You're still able to impress by your confident mocking and so on. But you know for sure how things really are.

And then… all of a sudden… I saw a completely different possibility and it's filled me with zest for life. I was in front of an abyss, paralyzed and afraid. I couldn't go back, didn't *want* that – it's not in my nature to retrace my steps, right? But forward was not possible either, because the abyss was gaping....

Suddenly I saw a bridge... far away, but not unreachable. I am that bridge myself, Maria – it must still be built. I feel the zest for work like never before! My whole life, all my memories, my knowledge... everything condenses and shows me the way to become the bridge myself. I must transform in true *knowledge*, gain a different, new content. That knowledge will be different from that of René, Maria or Johannes, even though it consists of the same words and concepts. It will have the colour, smell, quality, and order of *Agnes*. I shall find myself, Maria, and from there I'll build a bridge to the kingdom behind Death with all my energy and ambition. I shall overcome it because I shall invite it myself. At my invitation I shall go through it while my body is still alive. And when the moment comes when I have to discard it, it will be like taking off my coat. Death won't touch *me*! Oh Maria, I am so happy. Of course, I know that I'm up against powerful opponents. Besides death, there's another opponent, who lives inside me. But I shall overcome that opponent too because I shall transform its powers into a zest for work. Perhaps later, I'll soon feel despair because it'll all turn out to be so hard. Still, this moment, here and now, will stay with me. It'll be the light on my path. I love the whole world, Maria – and you most of all!'

Deeply touched, Maria looked at her. There, behind Agnes, she saw the human soul, the way it strives…. It lives in a thousand images, individual in each person … and still one in its striving for perfection. She, Maria, was named after the pure soul, but now she was seeing it manifold….

,*I see you in a thousand images,*
Mary, lovingly expressed.
But none of them can portray you
Quite like my soul contemplates you.

I only know that ever since that time,
The turmoils of this world are blown away like a dream,
And that an unnameable sweet heaven
Remains in my heart forever.'

Novalis, Geistliche Lieder.